OUR LADY AT GARABANDAL

by
Judith M. Albright

Queenship

P.O. Box 220
Goleta, CA 93116

The publisher recognizes and accepts that the final authority regarding the apparitions at Garabandal rests with the Holy See of Rome, to whose judgment we willingly submit.

-- The Publisher

Our Lady at Garabandal
Originally published by Faith Publishing Company © 1992

Copyright © 1992 Judith M. Albright

ISBN: 1-57918-139-2
Library of Congress Card No.: 92-075070

Photo Credits: The publisher gratefully acknowledges permission from Joey Lomangino for the use of the photographs from the quarterly magazine *GARABANDAL*. The magazine can be obtained at the yearly subscription rate of $15.00 from:

GARABANDAL
The Workers of Our Ladys of Mount Carmel
PO Box 606
Lindenhurst, New York 11757

Cover Photo: The inside of San Sabastian Church at Garabandal.

Published by:
    Queenship Publishing
    PO Box 220
    Goleta, CA 93116
    (800) 647-9882 / (805) 692-0043
    Fax (805) 967-5843

Printed in United States of America

Table of Contents

An artist's rendition of the Archangel Michael's first appearance to the girls on Sunday, June 18, 1961.

Dedication

This book is dedicated to all those who love Our Lady and say the Most Holy Rosary. I especially would like to dedicate this book to my family and to the memory of my parents Dr. and Mrs. Matthew McMahon and William and Frances Reck.— JMA

Our Lady of Mount Carmel at Garabandal.

Publisher's Statement

The second half of this century has produced the greatest array of visions, apparitions and supernatural manifestations the world has ever seen. It is no longer possible for the world, or the Church, to dismiss them as products of mass hysteria or over-active imaginations. They are too accurate. They are too identical in the messages being conveyed.

Perhaps lost in this great avalanche of heavenly messages is an event that occurred in the early 1960s. It was overshadowed at the time by other events that were capturing headlines: the great Vatican II Council which was destined to "re-energize" the Church, and a nasty little war in some place known as Vietnam. Additionally, the messages didn't seem to fit and weren't what the world wanted to hear.

It may be time to take another quick look at those apparitions. They occurred in a backward, remote little village named Garabandal, in northern Spain. Judith Albright has produced a simple, easy to read story of these events at Garabandal. We just now might be reaching the fulfillment of the messages allegedly given by the Blessed Virgin Mary to four young girls in that peasant village.

We believe it is important, as publisher of this work, to first state that Garabandal has its critics and its controversies. Much of the controversy over the events of Garabandal stemmed from two messages. The first gave some rather harsh admonishments to the ordained Church, predictions that have since proven extremely accurate. The second message spoke of tribulations and warnings and "the great miracle" and a coming chastisement.

These issues are no more resolved today than they were then, although they are admittedly much more in focus now, given the current state of the world and the Church. With all this in mind, the publisher states that we offer no endorsement of the claimed apparitions at Garabandal, nor do we claim any official sanction of the Church as to the messages given. The events at Garabandal have neither been approved nor condemned by the Church as of February 1999. We offer this book as an opportunity for the reader to be informed and to discern. May the Mother of Jesus Christ, our Savior, and her Spouse, the Holy Spirit, guide you accordingly.

The material presented herein is the history of the events as presented by the author.

THE RIEHLE FOUNDATION

Introduction

San Sebastian de Garabandal is a tiny village in northern Spain. It is in the province of Santander, about fifty miles southeast of the city of Santander. It is in the heart of the Cantabrian Mountains.

In 1961, the village consisted of seventy quaint, little, stone homes on the side of the mountain. The people were mostly farmers, although the land was rough and rocky and very difficult for growing crops. Cattle and sheep grazed in the open land areas, but the farms were very poor.

Garabandal was an extremely impoverished area. The poverty of the people was evident. They had few modern conveniences. They had no cars or modern farm equipment. There were no stores, paved streets or sidewalks.

The homes of Garabandal were very old and run down. There was no electricity or running water. People had to use fireplaces and old cook stoves to heat their homes in the wintertime. When snow came, they would be isolated from the rest of the world for weeks.

The villagers made their own clothing and grew their own food. They canned their food for the winter months. When they needed other supplies, they had to take a four mile trip down the mountainside. It was a narrow, rocky, dirt road leading to the city of Cosio.

Garabandal had a school with two small rooms, one for the boys and one for the girls. Education was not stressed in the village, however, and attendance at school was sporadic. In the winter it was often too cold to go to school, and in the spring the children were needed to help with the farm work.

As the children grew up, the young people would either remain at their family home and work as their parents had, or go to larger cities in Spain to find work. Some of the more adventurous youth would travel to Mexico or the United States to find jobs and make their homes.

Most of the people in Garabandal were Catholic. No priest lived in the village, but there was a Catholic Church. Every Sunday evening a priest would climb the mountain to say Mass. He would hear confessions before Mass. After Mass, the priest would walk back down the steep mountainside to his home in Cosio.

Garabandal had always been a very "Catholic" community. There was no daily Mass. Therefore, the villagers appreciated their Sunday Mass all the more. The people gathered in the Church of San Sebastian to recite the rosary every day. This practice continues to this day. Prayer has always been the center of family and community life.

Each year on July 18, the feast day of St. Sebastian, the people would have a big celebration. They would carry the statue of St. Sebastian around the village in procession. They would then put the statue in a place of honor and have a dinner and dance. When it was over, the statue would be returned to the church.

The people of Garabandal practiced many religious customs. Each evening at sunset a woman would walk through the village ringing a bell to remind the villagers to pray for the poor souls in Purgatory.

Every day, at noon, the church bell would ring and the

people would stop working to say the Angelus. Even those who were in the fields would hear the bell and stop to pray. They also said the Angelus at six o'clock in the evening.

The villagers had a statue of the Blessed Virgin that was passed from family to family where it would remain in a home for a certain period of time to encourage family prayer. It was considered an honor and a privilege to have this statue in the home.

Between June 18, 1961 and June 18, 1965, four young girls from Garabandal claimed to have received supernatural apparitions from Our Lady and Saint Michael. They said Our Lady came, as a mother, to warn her children to pray, to do penance and to be good because, as she told them, "the destiny of the world is at stake." Apparently, Our Lady appeared over 2,000 times, praying, teaching, comforting and leading the children to God.

The girls were also told that they would have much to suffer and they would have serious doubts later on as to whether or not the apparitions had actually occurred. This became one of the earliest prophecies of Garabandal to be fulfilled. The girls also received locutions from God and His Holy Mother, by which they could hear the voices within their hearts without actually seeing anyone.

The girls were young. Conchita Gonzalez, Mari Loli Mazon and Jacinta Gonzalez were twelve years old, and Mari Cruz Gonzalez was eleven. Conchita and Jacinta were second cousins.

People from all over the world soon heard about the apparitions at Garabandal and went to the small village. They watched the young girls and followed them as they walked about in their unusual trances during the times of the apparitions. They saw miracles occur and the girls perform impossible feats which led to many conversions.

People who went to Garabandal found themselves drawn into a deeper understanding of what the Mass is all about and, as a result, had a more special devotion to the Blessed Sacrament. They listened to the messages given by Our Blessed Mother and understood her love and concern for all children upon earth. They knew that her messages were important and that they must be made known so that people would understand that she is a loving mother who is trying to lead her children back to the Father.

On the road to Garabandal in 1961. L to R, Mari Cruz, Jacinta, Conchita, and Mari Loli.

While in ecstasy the children laugh and joyfully communicate with Our Lady. L to R, Mari Loli, Conchita, Jacinta, Mari Cruz.

The children instinctively ran to the village church after the vision of St. Michael.

Fr. Valentin Marichalar, Garabandal's pastor during the time of the apparitions.

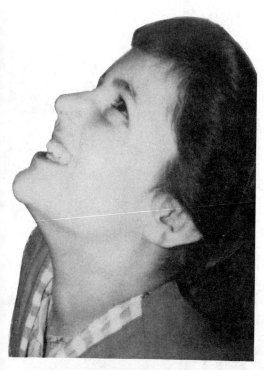

Caption 5

The girls experienced enhanced beauty during and immediately after ecstasy.

Mari Loli

Mari Cruz.

Conchita

Mari Loli seems to have received "two calls and something more" as she races to meet Our Lady. The three other visionaries accompany her but do not appear to have been called.

Mari Cruz and Jacinta run to see Our Lady after receiving their second "call" from the Virgin.

Conchita tries to stay awake waiting for a late "call" from the Virgin.

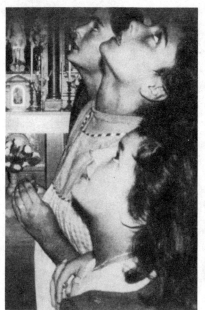
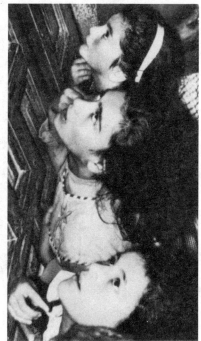

In the beginning the girls, while in ecstasy, would lead the crowds into the church. Under obedience to the Bishop, however, the Virgin began to lead the girls only as far as the church doors and not inside.

The girls, while in ecstasy, often positioned themselves in unusual ways. Mari Loli and Jacinta experience an ecstatic fall while inside the village church.

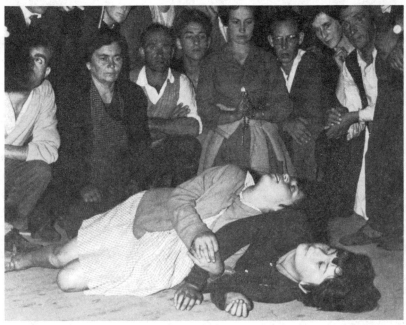

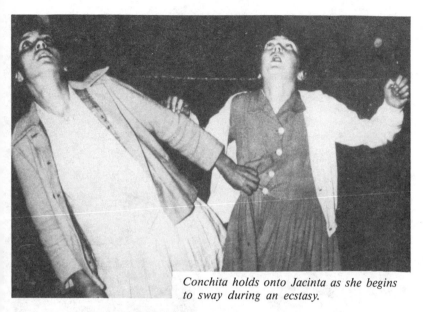

Conchita holds onto Jacinta as she begins to sway during an ecstasy.

A former weight lifter was not able to lift Mari Loli while she was in ecstasy.

Mari Loli easily lifts Jacinta so she can present the crucifix on her rosary for Our Lady to kiss.

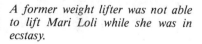

Jacinta, while in ecstasy, holds up a holy card for Our Lady to kiss.

Mari Loli, while in ecstasy, presents the crucifix for veneration.

These two photos laid side by side depict the visionaries in ecstasy. L to R, Jacinta and Mari Loli offer rosaries to Our Lady.

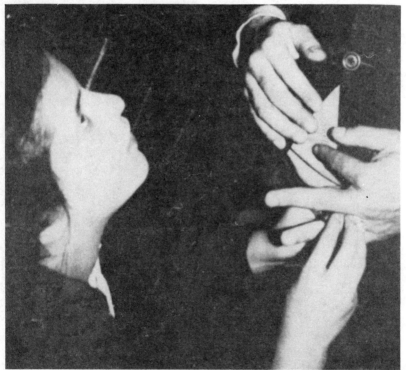

While in ecstasy, Mari Loli returns a "kissed" wedding ring to its rightful owner.

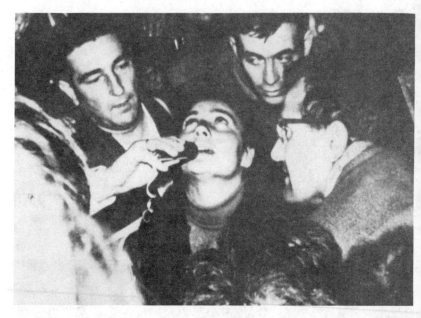

A microphone is held to Conchita's mouth while she is in ecstasy.

Conchita is confident as she answers questions from a priest.

Conchita, in ecstasy, is about to receive mystical communion from St. Michael the Archangel.

Conchita receives communion from St. Michael. The hosts were real and could be seen, tasted and swallowed by the visionaries. They remained invisible except for this one occasion.

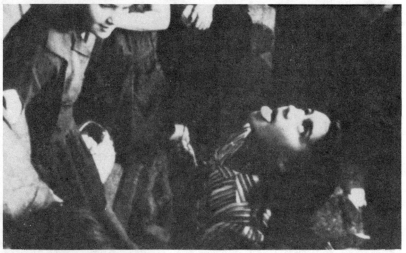

This frame of an 8 mm film shows the host on Conchita's tongue.

Conchita, along with her mother and brother, cuts grass on the mountain-side. This will serve as fodder for the animals during winter months.

Jesuit Fr. Alejandro, with Fathers Ramon and Luis Andreu and their mother who became a Visitation nun after Luis's death.

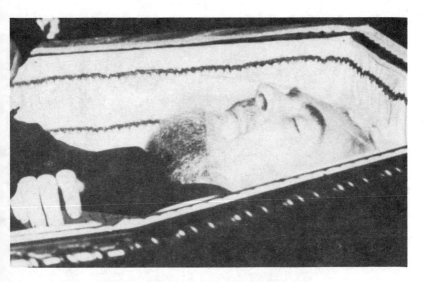

The veil covering Padre Pio's face was given to Conchita.

Conchita in July 1969, at age 20.

Pilgrims still climb the hill to the group of pine trees where Our Lady appeared many years ago to four little girls.

CHAPTER 1

The First Apparition

SUNDAY, JUNE 18, 1961

"Benedicat vos omnipotens Deus, Pater et Filius et Spiritus Sanctus," said Father Valentin Marichalar as he finished saying Mass.

"Amen," responded the people in the church.

"May almighty God bless you, the Father, the Son and the Holy Spirit. Amen."

The people left the church and gathered in the little village square as they did every Sunday evening. It was a time to socialize and catch up on the neighborhood gossip. The children followed their parents and began to play together.

"Let's climb the wall and go get some apples!" Conchita whispered to her friend Mari Cruz.

The two girls giggled quietly together for a while and then secretly moved around the corner of the stone building. When they were out of sight of the others, they raced across an open area and jumped over an old stone wall, where they reached their destination of a fruit-filled apple tree growing in the yard of the schoolteacher.

Unknown to Conchita and Mari Cruz, their friends Mari Loli and Jacinta had seen them sneak away and had followed them.

1

"Conchita, you're stealing apples," shouted Jacinta as she ran toward the girls.

"Hush! Be quiet," whispered Conchita. "If the teacher hears us, Mommy will find out."

Mari Cruz began to run away, but Mari Loli called after her, "Mari Cruz, we've already seen you, and we are going to tell the teacher."

Mari Cruz stopped running and slowly went back to the tree where the other girls were waiting. Before long, all four girls were picking apples and laughing.

"I think the sheep are eating our apples again!"

The girls heard the schoolteacher's loud voice. Fearing she would come out of the house and find them, the four girls ran away.

After they had finished eating the stolen apples, the girls began to feel sorry that they had taken them.

"I bet our poor guardian angels are sad because we took those apples," said Conchita.

"Yes," responded Mari Cruz, "and I bet the devil is very pleased with us."

"Let's throw stones at the wicked devil to get rid of him, and then our guardian angels will be happy again," said Jacinta. She picked up a stone and threw it to the left with all of her might. They believed that the good angels were on the right and the bad devils were on the left. The other girls copied this action until they got tired of throwing stones and then sat down to play something else.

The sound of thunder made them think that it was going to rain and that they should start for home.

Suddenly, to her amazement, Conchita saw a very bright, beautiful figure, surrounded by a brilliant light. Speechless, she pointed to the apparition.

The girls first looked at Conchita and were afraid that something was wrong with her, and then they looked to where she was pointing. They too saw the apparition.

"An angel!" they all exclaimed.

The girls looked at the angel but did not say another

word. The angel looked at them but did not say or do anything. Then he disappeared.

The four girls were very frightened. They ran toward the square where all of the people were still gathered. When they were near the church another friend saw them and was very concerned.

"What has happened to you!" she exclaimed. "You look pale and afraid. Where have you been?"

"We took some apples and we ate them," the girls confessed.

"Why do you look so scared?" the other girl questioned.

"We've seen an angel!" all four girls replied.

The girl did not know what to think. She ran off to tell their friends at the square.

By this time the four girls were at the Church but they were afraid to go inside. They went behind the Church and began to cry. They did not know what to do.

Someone had told the teacher, since she lived so close, and she approached the girls saying, "Did you really see an angel?"

"Yes," the girls answered.

"Is it true or did you just imagine that you saw an angel?" asked the teacher again.

"It is true," replied Conchita crying.

"The teacher knew the girls very well. She was sure that they would not lie, but she had to question them more. "What did he look like?"

He looked like a child. He was small, about nine years old, but he seemed very strong. He was wearing a long blue seamless robe. He had wings that were large and pinkish. His face was small and his eyes were black. The girls all agreed as they described the angel.

The teacher watched the girls, and when they were through talking, she really believed them. "Let's go into the church and say a station in thanksgiving to Jesus in the Blessed Sacrament," she said.

The teacher and the children went into the church to pray. A station was a common prayer said in that particular region of Spain in honor of the Seven Sorrows of Mary. It consisted of saying seven Our Fathers, seven Hail Marys and seven Glorias, plus an extra Our Father for the intention of the Holy Father.

When they finished praying they all went home. It was about nine o'clock at night, and by now it was very dark.

"Didn't I tell you to get home before dark?" asked Conchita's mother. She was angry with her daughter.

Quietly, Conchita leaned against the wall. "I have seen an angel," she said to her mother.

"What!" exclaimed her mother. "On top of coming home late, you now make up stories like that?"

"But it's true, mother. I have seen an angel."

Conchita's mother watched her daughter as they continued on with their normal activities of dinner and getting ready for bed. She noticed a quiet, serene attitude and wondered if all this could be possible.

Mari Loli found her sister, who was a year younger, and told her about seeing the angel. When the two girls went into their home, their mother was also waiting for them.

"What a time for you two to get home!" she exclaimed harshly. "I should beat both of you!"

"We are late because Loli has seen an angel!" said her sister.

"An angel? Not a devil? You should be ashamed of yourself! Now eat your dinner and get ready for bed!"

The same kind of anger and disbelief occurred in the homes of Jacinta and Mari Cruz. Each girl told her family about seeing an angel, but no one actually believed them.

When the girls went to bed that night, sleep was impossible. They had so many questions. One thing each girl felt for sure was that she had seen an angel.

CHAPTER 2

The Apparitions of the Angel

MONDAY, JUNE 19, 1961

The next day, everyone in the village was talking about the girls who had seen an angel. Some of the people believed them while others went out of their way to tease them.

"You must have seen a big bird."

"Maybe it was a boy from some other village."

"All of you were having the same dream!"

But when the people listened to the girls, while they were describing the angel, something changed and the doubts turned to wonder.

After the children went off to school, someone walked to Cosio to tell Father Valentin. The priest listened to the story and then felt that it was important enough for him to go back to Garabandal to talk with the girls.

He walked up the mountainside wondering what was going to happen, saying his rosary as he walked. He met Jacinta and Mari Cruz at one o'clock as they were on their way home from school.

"Is it true that you saw an angel?" he asked.

"Yes, Father," the girls responded together.

"Maybe you have made a mistake," the priest went on. "Tell me about it."

The two girls then explained to the priest everything

that had happened. He watched them intensely for their reactions as they described the angel. Father Valentin knew these girls but he also knew that he would have to be very careful with his examinations.

Next he found Conchita walking home and questioned her. "Conchita, be honest. What did you see last night?"

Conchita explained everything and he listened carefully.

"If you see the angel tonight, ask him who he is and why he has come," said the priest.

"Oh, yes, Father," agreed Conchita. She really felt that the priest believed them and would help them. These children had always been taught to respect priests, and Father Valentin had warm feelings for the people of Garabandal.

The priest then went to question Mari Loli and discovered that all of the girls fully agreed with each other. He was impressed with their straight answers. He decided that the best thing would be to wait and see what would happen. He kept very good documents, and he decided that if any more visions occurred, the Bishop would be notified.

The children returned to school in the afternoon and, after school, decided to go to the place where the angel had appeared to them. They called it the "calleja" which was a rocky lane leading to a group of pine trees on a hill.

First they went to their homes to get permission from their parents. These children were raised to be very honest and obedient.

"Mother, I am going to pray at the calleja," said Conchita.

"I don't know what to do. If it is true, I don't want to stop you," said her mother.

"Let her go," replied Conchita's older brother. "What harm is there in praying?"

They all agreed, and Conchita ran off to join the others. Some people gathered to watch the girls, and some even joined in with the rosary. Others continued to jeer and laugh.

The girls finished the rosary and waited for the angel. They finally decided that he was not going to come so they went to the church to make a visit to the Blessed Sacrament. Then they went to their homes.

"Did you see the angel?" asked Conchita's mother and brother.

"No, we did not see him today," answered Conchita.

That night, while Conchita was saying her night prayers she heard a voice say, "Don't worry. You shall see me again."

TUESDAY, JUNE 20, 1961

The next day things went as usual in Garabandal. The four girls again decided to go to the rocky lane to say the rosary in the evening. At first Conchita's mother told her that she could not go, but after a while, she let her daughter run to join the others. No one followed the girls this time.

The four little girls knelt down in the road and said the rosary. Again they waited for the angel. When he did not come, they decided to go home. As they were getting up from their knees, they saw a very bright light, and each girl was enveloped in a light where she could see nothing but the light. They were all terrified for a moment, but then the light disappeared and they were all fine.

Shaken by this unusual experience, the girls went right home. They did not want to talk to anyone, but they had promised the priest that if anything else happened they would tell him. The girls were not allowed to go to Cosio by themselves, so they knew they had to tell their parents so someone could tell the priest.

WEDNESDAY, JUNE 21, 1961

After school, the girls all went to their own homes and did their usual chores. Again they asked their parents if they could go to the rocky lane. This time they were accompanied by two women of the village, Clementina Gonzalez and her friend Concesa. Seeing the two adults with the children, others followed them. They all said a rosary.

When the rosary was finished and the angel had not appeared, someone suggested that they say a station. After the station, the angel appeared.

"Who are you, and why have you come here?" asked Conchita. She had remembered what the priest had told her to say.

The angel did not answer, but he looked at the girls with a pleasant smile on his face.

When the vision was over, all the people were excited. They believed the girls because they had seen their faces become visibly changed during the ecstasy. Their faces became very pale and transparent-like with an almost glowing effect. The girls had the most beautiful expressions on their faces.

Their entire beings suddenly changed. Each girl had become beautiful and assumed an attitude of beauty deep in prayer and devotion. They radiated a beauty which was impossible to describe and marvelous to witness. This was the only visible proof the villagers needed.

"It's true! It's true!" Clementina repeated over and over again. "An angel really has appeared to these little ones!"

Everyone was very excited and asked the children many questions.

THURSDAY, JUNE 22, 1961

The children continued the same pattern that had been established during the beginning of the week. They got up, went to school until one o'clock, returned home, then went back to school at three to finish their lessons, returned home again for their chores and then went to the rocky lane to say the rosary and wait for the angel.

This time the priest was with the crowd of people who had come to watch the children.

The angel again appeared after the rosary, and the people all began to shout and to say that truly the apparition was authentic. They could not see the angel, but they could tell by the faces of the girls in ecstasy that they were looking at a supernatural being.

FRIDAY, JUNE 23, 1961

A large crowd of people gathered with the priest to watch the children during their ecstasy. When it was over the priest took the four girls into the church to question them. He talked with each girl individually and again was impressed with their agreement of facts.

When the questioning was over, the priest went outside to make a statement. "I have questioned these four little girls together and alone, and they all agree in what they say they have seen. These children undoubtedly saw something that is not of this world. It might well be God's work."

Everyone was satisfied with Father Valentin's statement.

SATURDAY, JUNE 24, 1961

When the angel appeared to the girls this time he spoke one word. "Hay," which means "it is necessary that." He held a sign upon which were written Roman numerals.

"What do you mean?" asked Conchita.

"We don't understand," said Mari Loli.

The angel only smiled at them. He did not say another word or do anything to help the children understand the meaning of this apparition.

Later, when the priest asked them about the numerals, none of the girls knew what they were. They had been so interested in looking at the beauty of the angel that they did not pay much attention to the sign.

SUNDAY, JUNE 25, 1961

People came from all of the nearby villages as word of the visions spread. Five priests and many doctors came to examine the girls. The people of the village had built a little enclosure with posts and poles at the rocky lane to protect the girls from the crowds. It was called the "cuadro."

During the ecstasy, one doctor had Conchita lifted up in the air and dropped hard on her knees. People were sure that they heard the sound of bones breaking and were concerned about the child.

When the apparition was over, they pushed to see if Conchita was alright. Conchita did not understand what had happened, and her knees were perfectly fine. The girls did notice that their legs and arms had lumps and marks from pin pricks and pinches that they had received from the various tests of the doctors. They were surprised because they had felt no pain, but still the marks were there.

It was discovered that when the girls were in ecstasy they felt no outside physical pain. They were also not aware of anything that was going on around them. They could only see the angel and each other as long as they were all in the light of the angel. When the angel left, the girls were surprised that it was so dark outside. The light of the angel made everything bright, but it did not hurt their eyes.

WEDNESDAY, JUNE 28, 1961

The angel did not appear to the girls for two days, and the people began to wonder what had happened. But on Wednesday evening, at about nine o'clock, he appeared once again in the rocky lane after they had said the rosary.

When he appeared, the girls asked once again why he had come, but he just looked at them and smiled. This same thing happened for the next two days.

SATURDAY, JULY 1, 1961

Many people were at Garabandal for the apparition on Saturday. The girls said the rosary, and the angel appeared as usual, and the girls went into ecstasy. This time the angel talked with them.

"Do you know why I have come? It is to announce to you that tomorrow, Sunday, the Virgin Mary will appear to you as Our Lady of Mount Carmel."

The girls were so happy. From their expressions, the

people could see that something unusual was happening.

"Is that why you appeared to us—to tell us that the Blessed Virgin is coming?" asked Jacinta.

The angel smiled and appeared very happy. He had the sign with him again, and this time the girls asked him about it.

"The Blessed Virgin will tell you the meaning of the sign," he said.

The angel and the girls talked for two hours, but it seemed like a very short time to the girls. When he left he said, "I shall return tomorrow with the Blessed Virgin!"

The girls and the people were all happy as they walked back to the church. They were anxious to tell the priest what they had seen and heard. They sang songs and said the rosary in honor of Our Blessed Mother.

CHAPTER 3

Our Lady of Mount Carmel

SUNDAY, JULY 2, 1961
THE FEAST OF THE VISITATION

Excitement spread through the small village of Garabandal as everyone talked about the coming of the Blessed Virgin Mary. It seemed to these peasant people as if the whole world had come to their town.

The narrow streets were suddenly crowded with strangers pushing and shoving and asking questions. The Civil Guards, the Spanish country police, were out in uniform to escort the girls to the lane and to keep order as much as they could. Many priests and doctors had come to witness the event.

It was six o'clock in the evening, and the four little girls were together.

"Let's go to the lane where the angel appeared to us," said Mari Loli.

"Yes," said Jacinta. "If we go where they put up the barricade, we will be safe from all the people."

"Let's say a rosary when we get there so that the Blessed Virgin will know that we want her to come," said Conchita.

The streets became more hectic as the girls started to walk to the rocky lane. The guards helped the girls as they hurried along.

12

They stated that, suddenly, the Blessed Virgin Mary appeared in front of them! There was light all around her. Astonished, the girls looked at Our Lady for a long time and then noticed that there was an angel standing on either side of her. Although the angels looked alike, the children recognized one as St. Michael.

Our Lady had on a white robe and a blue mantle. Her white garment had faintly visible patterns of what looked like flowers. Her feet could not be seen.

On her head, she wore a crown with twelve small golden stars. In her hand she held a large Brown Scapular like the one of Our Lady of Mount Carmel. The scapular had a mountain on one part and a cross on the other. It was brown in color, but the cross was white.

She had long dark hair that went down to her waist. Her hair was parted in the middle. Her face was the most beautiful face the girls had ever seen. Words could not describe her beauty. Her nose was dainty, and her mouth was very pretty with slightly full lips. She was about seventeen years old. Her voice was sweet and pure, and all four girls said that there was no other voice like hers!

"I am the Lady of Mount Carmel!" she said.

The girls saw a strange symbol on the right side of Our Lady, parallel with her head. They saw a square of red fire which framed a triangle containing a large eye. They also saw some type of writing which they were unable to read. Later people said that this was a symbol of God, and the triangle meant the Blessed Trinity.

The four little girls were not afraid or shy when they were in the presence of Our Lady. They all began to chat as if she were a friend that they had not seen for a long time.

Our Lady, apparently pleased with the simple little girls, smiled a lot and asked them questions and answered their questions in a very easy manner. As a mother, she listened lovingly to their childish stories and showed her Motherly love and concern for everybody when she said, *"I have come for all my children."*

Our Lady identified the angel who had appeared to the girls as St. Michael the Archangel.

"I've got a brother called Michael, too, but without the saint part," said Jacinta.

The girls giggled at this response and Our Lady smiled.

"Everyone is behind with the hay-making," Conchita confided to Our Lady. "The hay is still piled and waiting to be spread to dry."

The children explained how they did their chores and what else needed to be done.

Finally Our Lady asked the girls to pray with her. They recited a rosary together, and Our Lady taught them how to say it well, slowly and meditating on the mysteries. When the rosary was finished, she told them that she was leaving.

"Oh, please don't go!" begged Conchita.

"You have only been with us for a short time," said Mari Cruz. "We want you to stay longer."

"I shall return tomorrow," said the Blessed Virgin. She was so kind and gentle with the girls. She looked at them once again and smiled. Then she disappeared.

"She's gone," said the girls. They were filled with mixed emotions. The girls felt very sad because Our Lady had left but so happy because she had come.

They had seen the Blessed Virgin Mary for the first time, and they had immediately fallen in love with her. All they wanted to do was to look at her and pray with her and do whatever she wished.

When the ecstasy was over, all of the people tried to reach the children to touch them and kiss them. Some of the people believed immediately; others did not. Those people who believed said that the apparition was like a mother coming to see her daughters whom she had not seen for a long time.

The children were pushed and shoved and finally brought to the church, where the priest interviewed them. Other priests were there too and asked many questions.

Thus began a series of apparitions of Our Lady that was longer than any recorded up to that time. It is claimed Our Lady appeared to the girls over 2,000 times in the following four years.

CHAPTER 4

Blessings and Miracles

By appearing on the feast of the Visitation, the Blessed Virgin was stressing the importance of what had occurred many years before when Mary went to visit her cousin Elizabeth. Elizabeth was the first to recognize Mary as the Mother of God, and she was the first to speak the words, *Blessed art thou among women and blessed is the fruit of thy womb* (*Luke* 1:42-43).

Our Lady wanted the world to know that she is the Mother of God, and she also wanted to bring her Son to the world so that the people of the world could know Him, love Him and serve Him, as He so rightly deserves.

Our Lady prayed the rosary with the girls and taught them to pray it with meaning. They didn't just hurry through the prayers but spoke very slowly so that they could think about the words and meditate on the mysteries. In this way she could teach them about her Son.

The second day Our Lady appeared in Garabandal, she presented her Son to the world by actually bringing the Christ Child with her. The four little girls were surprised and thrilled when they saw Our Lady holding the Baby.

They described Him as being an infant, but when He looked at them He seemed to know them completely. The Blessed Virgin smiled, and so did Jesus.

The girls, being very simple and not realizing the magnitude of the apparitions, entertained the small child with little games and kisses. They picked up rocks for Him to play with. When they handed the small pebbles up for Baby Jesus, Our Lady touched and kissed them and told the girls to give the pebbles to the people.

When the people saw the girls holding rocks up to where Our Lady apparently was, they began to give the girls rosaries, medals and other holy objects for Our Lady to kiss. Our Lady seemed to like the idea, and the girls claimed she kissed objects that were presented to her.

This was the beginning of a pattern which was carried out for the next four years. At first, the villagers and people who came to watch the girls were mere observers, but that changed quickly.

Everyone soon joined in the recitation of the rosary and participated in giving objects for Our Lady to kiss. People would give the girls blessed wedding rings, medals, rosaries and crucifixes and even hang rosaries and medals around their necks.

There were so many people and so many items that it would seem impossible for the girls to know what item belonged to which person. But it was amazing how the girls were able to return the articles to the rightful owners during ecstasies.

Each item kissed by Our Lady was returned to the proper owner by a visionary while still in ecstasy. Their eyes were staring at the vision the whole time as the girls would go through the crowd of people until they reached the right person.

There were so many chains and rosary beads, but they never got tangled or lost. The girls never made a mistake, although many times priests and people tried to trick the girls. In fact, this act convinced many people that Our Lady was actually appearing to the girls because it was performed in a most supernatural way.

Only objects with a religious connotation were kissed by Our Lady. Someone questioned the kissing of wedding rings, but a priest was quick to point out that the wedding rings symbolized a sacrament of God, plus the fact that wedding rings are always blessed during the wedding ceremony.

The people also noticed that the girls would always return the wedding ring to the right person and place it on the correct finger. Different countries have different customs as to which finger and which hand the wedding ring is worn. Whatever that person's custom was, Our Lady followed that custom.

Many people left items to be kissed at the homes of the visionaries. One day, Conchita found a beautiful powder compact among the religious items. She questioned why it was there, and some other people wondered too, because it seemed to be so out of place. It was an item of decoration rather than something religious.

To everyone's suprise, when the apparition began, the very first thing Conchita picked up was the compact. Conchita said that Our Lady was especially pleased and said, *"Hand me that. It belongs to my Son."*

It was later learned that the compact had been used as a pyx to carry consecrated hosts. During the Spanish Civil War, a priest hid Holy Communion inside the compact and secretly brought it to prisoners who were going to be executed.

Many times people would notice the sweet smell of roses coming from an object kissed by Our Lady. This phenomenon has occurred many different times at many holy places.

At other times the girls would hold up a crucifix and Our Lady would kiss it and then direct the girls to present the crucifix to a certain person. Our Lady would say, *"Have* (Name) *kiss the crucifix,"* and the children would repeat the name.

The people in the crowd would immediately make way for that person to go to the girls and kiss the crucifix.

This was always considered an honor, because the person was actually selected by the Blessed Virgin.

Later someone asked Conchita of what value or power these objects kissed by the Blessed Virgin contained.

"The Blessed Virgin said that Jesus would perform miracles through objects kissed by her and that those who wear them with faith and confidence would make their Purgatory on this earth with suffering corresponding to what they would have endured in Purgatory," Conchita explained.

Conchita said Our Lady told her that the kissing of religious articles is very important. God bestows special graces upon those who believe and have faith. Many physical cures and conversions have been obtained by simply touching the objects kissed by Our Lady.

Our Lady also told Conchita that she does not perform miracles. Only God can perform miracles, and her Son performs miracles through those objects she has kissed.

Spiritual conversions became a significant factor in the apparitions at Garabandal. So many people had actually "turned their lives around" and began to live for God, that those studying the apparitions were reminded of the Bible verse, *By their fruits you shall know them.*

The physical healings are also important, for some people actually need to see a visible change in order to believe. Many miraculous cures throughout the world have taken place due to the religious items that Our Lady kissed. Hundreds of miracles are being studied that have been attributed to Our Lady at Garabandal.

CHAPTER 5

Actions of the Girls

When the four girls first experienced visions they would fall to their knees in a state of ecstasy. They were able to remain kneeling on stones and rocks for extremely long periods of time without moving.

The girls looked in the same direction and focused on the same spot. At times, as they looked up to Our Lady, their heads were tilted back in very awkward positions that would be impossible to maintain in any other circumstance.

Their eyes did not blink, although their faces showed various expressions of happiness and wonderment. When they came out of the ecstasy, they were relaxed and comfortable and at peace.

During an apparition the girls could see each other and Our Lady, but they were not aware of anything else that was going on around them. They said that they could only see whatever was in the light that came from the Blessed Virgin.

Doctors tested the reflexes, heartbeats, eyes, ears, noses and sensitivity to pain of the girls while they were in ecstasy. They did not react to any outside stimuli.

They were pinched and poked and even had needles stuck into their bodies, but they did not feel a thing. Bright lights were shined in their eyes during some of the nightly apparitions, but they did not blink or respond in any way. They were lifted up in the air by a group of strong men and dropped in such a way that would have hurt anyone in a normal state.

All of these tests proved that something extraordinary was occurring. Their actions and absence of reaction could not be explained by any scientific means. Even the heat of the summer or the cold of the winter did not affect them in any way during an ecstasy.

Sometimes the girls' voices could be heard by people close to them as they talked with Our Lady. Their voices were not their normal voices but more like husky whispers. Many of their conversations were recorded on a tape recorder or written down by someone who was close enough to hear.

Sometimes when the girls recited the Hail Mary while in ecstasy, they could be heard saying "...Holy Mary, Mother of God and our Mother, pray for us sinners..."

The girls began saying the Hail Mary like this together. No one told them to add "...and our Mother," but they all did it at the same time. Our Lady told them that she liked the prayer very much but that they should not use the new phrase with other people unless it was approved by the Church.

The apparitions occurred in many different places. In the beginning they were at the rocky lane, and then at the church. The girls had apparitions at the church door, around the church and at the cemetery. They occurred in various streets of the village and in the homes. It is said that Our Lady appeared in every home in Garabandal at one time or another. One of the favorite places for the apparition was at the pine trees. They said that the pines is the site where the future miracle will occur.

The girls would have their apparitions at various times throughout the day or night. Some days they had more than one apparition, and they would occur if the girls were together or alone.

There was no set time for the apparitions to begin or to end. The length of the apparitions varied from a few minutes to a number of hours. Time stood still for the girls, and they were always surprised when Our Lady would tell them that she had to leave. The apparition may have lasted for over an hour, but for the girls, it was just a matter of a few moments.

Although the girls never knew for sure when an apparition would occur, they did receive three inner warnings as signals which they called the "llamadas" or "callings" before each apparition.

First it was a slight feeling of joy and anticipation. The second call was more like an overflowing of happiness with a great desire. The third calling was an urgent feeling, and the girls would rush to the place for the apparition.

One day, Father Valentin decided to test the girls and see if they received these callings at the same time and if they would arrive at the rocky lane together, even if they were separated.

He had Mari Loli and Jacinta stay at one home while Mari Cruz and Conchita stayed at Conchita's home at the other side of the village. The girls did not know that the parish priest was testing them.

They all received the first calling, but they stayed in the two separate homes because it was usually more than an hour between the first and second calling. The girls received the second calling and became more excited and happy and anxious for the apparition.

Finally they received the third call, and the two pairs of girls dashed out of the homes and ran immediately to the rocky lane, arriving there at exactly the same time and falling to their knees in ecstasy. The priest was amazed and recorded all that had taken place.

A very unusual phenomenon began to occur when the girls were in the trance. They had what the priest called "ecstatic falls." At first, Mari Loli was seen swaying back and forth and suddenly jerked, as if she were going to fall. Jacinta was kneeling right next to her and reached out to help her friend. Then Mari Loli and Jacinta both were suddenly thrown backward to the ground simultaneously. Everyone who witnessed this became very fearful that the girls were injured. The girls remained in an unconscious state as they continued to have the vision. When the vision was over, they immediately returned to normal and stood up unharmed.

The ecstatic falls began to occur with all of the girls, and witnesses said that the girls were always in complete synchronization. They would fall and move their heads and arms in exactly the same manner at the same time.

Later, the girls began to have "estatic walks" where they would actually walk while they were in the trance. This was first recorded on August 5, 1961. During these walks the girls would have their heads tilted backward in a most unusual position, and it was impossible for them to see the ground in front of them. Later, they said that they were looking at the Virgin Mary the entire time. The girls would walk together, arm in arm, either frontward or backward at an incredible speed. They did not appear to be uncomfortable or in any distress as they walked with ease and agility.

The girls would speed up mountainous regions that were very difficult to climb, or up and down the rocky streets and hills of the village, day or night. They were often led to the grove of pine trees situated on a hill that overlooked the village.

Villagers would follow the girls, but would end up running trying to keep up with them. The parents were fearful that the girls would trip and hurt themselves.

One day Conchita's brother Miguel tried to keep up with the girls. He was surprised that an eighteen-year-old boy could not run as fast as three twelve-year-old girls who were holding onto each other's arms. The girls did not seem to be actually running; it was more like they were gliding and using no force. When they reached the site of the apparition, the girls were not tired at all, while Miguel arrived panting and out of breath.

The walk would stop instantly, some said, defying the laws of physics. The girls were never hurt during these walks and were never tired or out of breath. When doctors examined them they found their heart rate to be normal.

Sometimes during their night "estatic walks" the girls would enter the homes of the villagers and bless the children while they were sleeping in their beds. Other times they would awaken them and offer the crucifix to be kissed.

For penance, the girls went to the lane to pray early in the morning. Conchita started walking around the village late at night with her brother, saying the rosary. Many of the villagers would join her, even in the harsh winter weather.

"The Blessed Virgin always wants us to do penance," said Conchita.

Although the girls would often ask Our Lady to perform a miracle so that others would believe, they never seemed to worry, and they never tried to convince anyone about the apparitions. When asked why they were so calm about it, the response was that Our Blessed Virgin told them that those who did not believe would believe in the end.

Sometimes, while in ecstasy, the girls would walk around the streets of the village barefoot. There were sharp rocks, glass and all kinds of dangerous objects in the roads. The girls were never cut or harmed in any way. One time Conchita walked across some burning coals that someone had thrown out of their house, and she was not harmed. A doctor examined her feet, and to his amazement, there were no cuts, burns or bruises, and her feet were very clean. This was impossible for anyone walking in the dirty village streets.

The four girls often received kisses from the Blessed

Virgin. Many times at the end of an apparition the girls would be seen lifting each other up, without any difficulty, to receive a kiss from Our Lady.

When the girls were not in ecstasy and they would try to lift each other up, they would struggle and fall, laughing like all children, but during an ecstasy they lifted each other up with ease. If, however, during an ecstasy someone else tried to move them or lift them, it was very difficult.

When the four girls were not in ecstasy, they were completely normal and did the things that the other youth of Garabandal had always done. They went to school and helped in the fields. They did their home chores and played with their friends.

At times their normal childhood activities would become impossible because of the great number of pilgrims who went to Garabandal to pray and see the children to whom Our Lady was appearing.

In situations that might have been chaotic and caused confusion, everyone marveled at how the girls were always calm and poised. They had an aura of true peace. Their patience and meekness was beyond what would normally be endured. People loved to be with the girls. Their peace was contagious, and people felt good when they were near them.

The girls felt a deep longing for prayer and spent many more hours at prayer than they had before the apparitions. The people who went to Garabandal also began to pray and sacrifice more as they all began to live the messages of Our Lady.

CHAPTER 6

The Messages

From the first claimed apparition of Our Lady in Garabandal, many significant features were evident. She appeared as Our Lady of Mount Carmel holding the scapular. Our Lady of Mount Carmel has become a symbol of motherly protection, faith and conversion. It has been said that one day through the rosary and the scapular, the world will be saved.

When the Blessed Virgin Mary appears on earth she does not come just to entertain and make people believe that someone is actually seeing a vision. The most important aspect of any apparition is the message that Our Lady brings to us.

God made us to know Him, to love Him and to serve Him in this world and to be happy with Him in the next. God loves us. God sends the Blessed Virgin Mary to the world as our mother, to show us the way to her Son and back to God. When we are in serious danger, she comes to help us and to guide us as a mother. Mary always brings warnings, but she also brings solutions.

There were two formal messages given to the world by Our Lady at Garabandal. The first message was given to all four girls on July 4, 1961. The second message was given to Conchita on June 18, 1965, by St. Michael under the direction of the Blessed Virgin.

On July 4, 1961, during the third apparition, Our Lady asked the girls, *"Do you know the meaning of the sign that was beneath the angel?"*

"No, we don't," answered the girls.

"It had a message that I am going to give you in order that you may announce it publicly on the eighteenth of October." Our Lady told the girls that:

> We must make many sacrifices, perform much penance, and visit the Blessed Sacrament frequently. But first, we must lead good lives. If we do not, a chastisement will befall us. The cup is already filling up, and if people do not change, a very great chastisement will come upon us.

The second message of the Blessed Virgin Mary, on June 18, 1965, was given to Conchita for the world through the intercession of St. Michael.

> *As my message of October 18 has not been complied with and has not been made known to the world, I am advising you that this is the last one.*
>
> *Before, the cup was filling up. Now it is flowing over.*
>
> *Many cardinals, many bishops and many priests are on the road to perdition and are taking many souls with them.*
>
> *Less and less importance is being given to the Eucharist.*
>
> *You should turn the wrath of God away from yourselves by your efforts. If you ask His forgiveness with sincere hearts, He will pardon you.*
>
> *I, your mother, through the intercession of Saint Michael the Archangel, ask you to amend your lives.*
>
> *You are now receiving the last warnings.*

I love you very much and do not want your condemnation.

Pray to us with sincerity and we will grant your requests.

You should make more sacrifices. Think about the passion of Jesus.

At Garabandal Our Lady said, *"You must lead good lives."* She tells us to pray every day, especially to pray the rosary. Through rosary recitation and meditation we will be able to know and love Jesus Christ better. Our Lady stresses Mass, Holy Communion and visits to the Blessed Sacrament. *"My Son is there,"* she told the girls. Meditate on the passion of Christ. We must do penance and make sacrifices for sinners. We must pray for priests because they have the power to lead souls to Christ.

There were many other messages given to the girls by the Blessed Virgin. In 1962, she told Conchita that there would be only two more popes after Pope Paul VI and that one of the popes would have a very short reign. But this does not mean that the world will come to an end.

Our Lady told the girls to pray very much for the intention of the Holy Father. She said that all humanity would be within one Church, the Catholic Church, but, *"you must first pray very much for this unity."* Jacinta said that it was important to pray for this intention.

Our Lady talked with the girls about priests during the early phase of the apparitions. She taught them to love and respect priests, but more importantly, she taught them to pray for priests so that they may be holy and lead others to holiness.

"Conchita," Our Lady once said, *"I have not come for your sake alone. I have come for all my children, so that I may draw them closer to our Hearts."*

The Blessed Virgin warned the four little girls that they would have much to suffer. She said that later they would contradict each other and that their parents would not get along well with each other. There would come a time when each girl would doubt that she had even seen the apparitions and would even deny seeing the Blessed Virgin.

"How is it that one day we will say we did not see you, since we are seeing you now?" asked Conchita. The girls were astonished that Our Lady would say such a thing.

Although Our Lady knew that the girls would have much to suffer, she hoped this knowledge would alleviate their future confusion. Her warnings and predictions were the result of her motherly love.

Mary always calls us to change our hearts and turn our lives over to her Son, Jesus Christ. She wants us to convert by changing our lives. She warns that there could be a chastisement, but we still have time to avoid this punishment. She wants to lead us to her Divine Son, who in His Divine Mercy will shelter us.

Conchita wrote to Father Alba of Barcelona:

> The Blessed Virgin told me on January 1, 1965, that we Catholic Christians do not think about the other world, Heaven or Hell. She said that we should think about them and that if we did, our lives would be united with Christ. She also said that we should think and meditate more on the passion of Jesus. We should not only do this ourselves, but we should also see to it that others do likewise. This would bring us close to the happiness of God and we would accept our crosses with joy and for the love of God.

Conchita said that at each apparition Our Lady stressed the importance of saying the rosary each day. She said that the rosary was a very important part of the Message of the Blessed Virgin. We are also encouraged to make sacrifices out of our daily duties and offer up little things to the Lord.

Conchita states Our Lady said that we should pray fervently for our brothers and sisters who do not know God. We should also pray for those who do not express their gratitude for the graces they have received.

Loli, in ecstasy, has her pulse checked by a doctor.

CHAPTER 7

Warning, Miracle and Chastisement

Predictions of future events for the world were listed as part of the messages given by the Blessed Virgin. The first event will be a "warning" that will be for everyone. Next the great "miracle" (a permanent sign) will occur at the pines which grow near the village of Garabandal. If the warning and the miracle do not change the people and turn them to God, then a chastisement is predicted to occur.

WARNING

Conchita said that on January 1, 1965, at the pines, Our Lady told her about a "warning" that would be given to the world. This warning would be given before the miracle so that the world might amend itself and therefore alleviate the chastisement.

"This warning, like the chastisement, is a very fearful thing for the good as well as for the wicked," said Conchita. "It will draw the good closer to God, and it will warn the wicked that the end of time is coming and that these are the last warnings. No one can stop it from happening. It is certain, although I know nothing concerning the day or the date."

The year of the warning was revealed to Mari Loli but she is not allowed to talk about it at this time.

The warning will be seen and experienced everywhere and by everyone. It will be felt interiorly by every person on earth. It will be like a personal judgment, where we shall see the consequences of the sins we have committed.

Many people have interviewed Conchita and asked her about the warning. She could not tell about it in its entirety, but she could say that it will come directly from God and will be experienced by everyone in the whole world.

Exerpts from three interviews with Conchita follows:

Interview with Conchita (1965)

Q. What will the Warning be like?

A. The Warning will be like a revelation of our sins. It will be experienced by believers and non-believers and people of any religion whatsoever.

Q. Will the Warning be recognized and accepted by the world as a direct sign from God?

A. Certainly. I believe it is impossible that the world could be so hardened as not to change. The Warning is like a purification for the Miracle.

Q. What about the many people who do not know Christ; how will they understand the Warning?

A. For those who do not know Christ (non-Christian), they will believe it is a Warning from God.

(1973)

Q. What will occur on the day of the Warning?

A. The most important thing about that day is that everyone in the whole world will see a sign, a grace or a punishment within themselves—in other words, a warning. They will find themselves all alone in the world no matter where they are at the time, alone with their conscience right before God. They will then see all their sins and what their sins have caused.

Q. Will we all feel it at the same time?

A. Yes.

Q. How long will it last, a half hour, an hour?

A. I really don't know. I think that five minutes would be an adequate time.

Q. How will we feel it?

A. We will all feel it differently because it will depend on our conscience. The Warning will be very personal, therefore, we will all react differently to it. The most important thing will be to recognize our own sins and the bad consequences of them. You will have a different view of the Warning than me because your sins are different from mine.

Q. Will physical harm come upon me as a result of my sins?

A. No, not unless something results from the shock of the experience.

Q. So it will bring no physical harm but will consist of facing God alone with my sins. How about the good things; will I see them also?

A. No. This will be only a Warning to see your sins. It will be like a purification before the time of the Miracle to see if, with the Warning and the Miracle, we (meaning the whole world) will be converted.

(1977)

Q. Would you summarize for us what you know about the Warning?

A. What I remember is that the Virgin Mary told me that God will be sending us a Warning so as to purify us or prepare us to see the Miracle, and in this way we may draw enough grace to change our lives toward God. She told me what the Warning will consist of but not the date. I am not able to say what it consists of, but I am able to say what it will be like, more or less. It is a phenomenon which will be seen and felt in all the world; I have always given as an example that of two stars that collide. This phenomenon will not cause physical damage, but it will horrify us, because at that very moment, we will see our souls and the harm we have done. No one will have doubts of it being from God.

Q. Do you have any words of advice for the people in order that they might prepare for this event?
A. We must always be prepared with our souls in peace and not tie ourselves down so much to this world. Instead, we must think very often that we are here to go to Heaven and to be saints.

According to Conchita, the warning will be a personal experience where each person will become aware of one's own sins and experience a deep remorse for them along with a desire to amend one's life.

Conchita said, "I think that those who do not despair will experience great good from the warning for their sanctification."

Jacinta said that the warning will affect the whole world. It will be of a short duration. Everything will come to a standstill. It will cause a shock as it brings to each one a vivid vision of one's life and where that person stands with God.

MIRACLE

Conchita also announced that there would be a public miracle, performed at the pines area, which would be so spectacular that all would believe. She is not allowed to tell what the miracle will be, but she will be able to announce the date of the miracle eight days before it is due to occur. Supposedly, the miracle will take place within 12 months of the warning.

Conchita was permitted to tell that the miracle will coincide with an event in the Church and with the feast of a saint martyr of the Eucharist. The miracle will take place at eight-thirty on a Thursday evening. It will be visible to all those who are in the village and the surrounding areas. The sick who are present will be cured and sinners will be converted.

"There will be no doubt in the mind of anyone who sees this great miracle which God, Our Lord, will perform through the intercession of the Blessed Virgin," said

Conchita. "It will be a miracle of the love of God, something that will prove and manifest His love to us in an outstanding way."

There will not be the slightest doubt that it comes from God and that it is for the good of mankind. A sign of the miracle, which will be able to be photographed, but not touched, will remain forever at the pines. The miracle is for the whole world.

Conchita is the only one to whom Our Lady revealed the year and date of the miracle.

CHASTISEMENT

Conchita explained that the Blessed Virgin told her that Jesus is not going to send the chastisement to discourage us, but to help us and to reprimand us for not heeding Him.

The chastisment is conditional and can be avoided if the world heeds the messages of the Blessed Virgin. Conchita has seen the chastisement and warns that when it comes it will be worse than being enveloped in fire.

"If we do not change, the chastisement will be terrible in keeping with what we deserve. When I saw it, I felt great fear, and that notwithstanding, I was looking at the Blessed Virgin."

Our Lady revealed to Conchita what the punishment would be, but she was not allowed to tell anyone, except that it will be an effect of God's Divine intervention, which makes it more fearful than anything imaginable.

Mari Loli and Jacinta were also given a preview of the chastisement during a vision on June 21, 1962. This vision occurred at night at the pines. They were accompanied by many people who heard the girls scream in terror. They saw the girls make gestures with their hands as if to ward off some frightening danger. Everyone sensed the danger and began to pray.

The next night, Mari Loli, Jacinta and Conchita all had the same vision. Mari Cruz was not present and did not witness the event. Again the girls began to scream, and again the people began to pray. As the prayers increased the screams of the girls decreased, but as soon as the praying stopped the cries were louder and more terrifying.

This event made a permanent impression upon the people who witnessed the three girls in this unusual ecstasy. It changed their lives. Everyone in the village went to confession the next day and resolved never to commit serious sin again.

Jacinta said that the chastisement would be subject to mankind's behavior, but if it comes, it will be terrible. It will not be a war, because war is caused by man. It will be something coming directly from God.

Conchita said that there is no use believing in the apparitions if we do not comply with the message and what our Holy Mother asks of us.

CHAPTER 8

Father Luis Andreu

The first time that Father Luis Andreu visited Garabandal he was with his brother Father Ramon, who was also a Jesuit priest. The two priests had gone to Garabandal out of curiosity as they really neither believed nor disbelieved in the apparitions.

Mari Loli and Jacinta had an apparition at the pines that day, and the two brother priests were near the girls while they were in ecstasy.

Father Ramon began to have serious doubts while watching the children and he thought to himself, "If this is authentic, let the apparition cease for one of them."

At that very moment Mari Loli came out of her trance and looked at Father Ramon and smiled.

"You aren't seeing the Blessed Virgin any more?" he asked.

"No, sir," responded Mari Loli.

"And why?" asked the priest.

"Because she has gone," responded the little girl.

"Look at Jacinta," said the priest. "She is still seeing the vision."

Mari Loli turned and looked at Jacinta who was very much in ecstasy. It was the first time that Mari Loli had seen one of her friends in that position, and she smiled.

"What did the Blessed Virgin tell you?" asked Father Ramon.

But just at that moment, Mari Loli returned to the position with her head tilted back, and she too was in ecstasy.

Father Ramon was close enough to hear the girls speak in the low, guttural voices that they used during the apparitions.

"Loli, why did you leave?" Jacinta asked her friend. During apparitions the girls were aware of each other as long as they were in the light that came from Our Lady. Loli had gone out of the light, and Jacinta was aware of her absence.

Mary Loli then asked Our Lady, "Why did you leave?" There was a pause while Mari Loli listened to Our Lady's answer. Father Ramon then heard Mari Loli say, "Oh! That's why? It was so he would believe!"

When Father Luis heard his brother's story he became very enthusiastic about the apparitions at Garabandal. He was happy when he was able to return to the village on August 8, 1961, with a group of people. The pastor had asked Father Luis to substitute for him for the day and had given him the keys to the church.

When the group arrived in Garabandal, they went directly to the Church so that Father Luis Andreu could say Mass. Jacinta and Mari Loli attended Mass and received Holy Communion.

Father Luis Andreu was a very holy priest and always celebrated Mass with great devotion. The people who attended this Mass commented upon how exceptionally pious the priest was and how they were all able to become more reverent by his example. Some thought that this was due to the fact that the visionaries were in attendance.

Later, after his unusual death, people wondered if perhaps Father Luis had some kind of a premonition that this was going to be his last Mass, and that is why he said it with such deep devotion.

After Mass, the two girls told the priest and the people

that Our Lady had announced a vision for all four visionaries in the church at noon.

Father Luis and two other priests stayed close to the
four little girls when they entered the church at twelve
o'clock for the vision. The priests were prepared to docu-
ment the entire encounter and wanted to be close enough
to hear the girls when they spoke.

At 12:10 the girls went into ecstasy. Their faces became
radiant, and their heads were tilted backward in the usual
position.

Conchita asked Our Lady for a public miracle so that
others would believe them. "At Lourdes and Fatima you
gave them proof. . ." She then smiled and changed the
subject. "Do you want me to show you what I've got?"

Holding up several rosaries for Our Lady to see, Conchita asked, "Will you kiss them for the people?"

The other girls also had rosaries and medals to be
kissed, and the conversations continued in very simple,
childlike fashion. Father Luis recorded questions and
statements that the girls made. He noted how the dialogue
was so simple, but yet it stressed the amazing familiarity
and naturalness of the children's conversation with their
Blessed Mother. He wrote that it should serve as an example to us all.

"Someone brought us some dolls". . ."How do you like
me with my hair cut short?". . ."You're coming again this
evening? Oh, how lovely!". . ."Do we have to stay two in
each house again this afternoon?". . ."Why haven't the angels returned again?". . ."There are some new priests who
have come here for the first time. One of them said Mass
very slowly and very nicely."

"When we ask you for proof, why do you look so
grave?" Conchita asked again. "It is nearly two months
now."

"Give it now, right away," Mari Loli pleaded. "You always say you will give it in time, in time."

The girls then made their ecstatic march backward to

the altar of Our Lady of the Most Holy Rosary and said
the rosary after they all fell to their knees in unison.
Father Luis commented on how beautifully the rosary was
said.

The apparition ended with Our Lady telling the girls
that she would appear to them in the evening at the pines.
The people were invited to go to the pines to pray and
observe the girls.

That evening all four girls went to the church where
they fell into ecstasy. Again Father Luis heard them and
wrote down the words they spoke. "Yes, as you
wish". . ."As you command". . ."We haven't been given
any proof yet". . ."People don't believe". . ."I don't mind
going all over the place". . ."Anything you say. . ." The
girls would pause to listen to the Blessed Virgin. Only the
words of the children could be heard.

The girls rose in unison and began their ecstatic march
to all of the places where the Virgin had appeared. They
ended up at the pines where they knelt and sang a hymn.
They kissed something in the air.

Suddenly, Father Luis Andreu turned pale, he too went
into ecstasy. "A miracle!" he shouted. "A miracle! A
miracle!"

The four girls could see Father Luis. They were surprised because they had never been able to see anyone
while in ecstasy except for Our Lady, baby Jesus, the angels and each other.

They immediately asked the Blessed Virgin why they
could see Father Luis, and she explained to them that he
could see her and that he was seeing the miracle.

"You will soon be with me," the girls heard Our Lady
say as she looked at the priest.

The girls continued to be in ecstasy and went down the
hill from the pines as if they had wings on their heels.
Mari Loli and Conchita led the rosary as they walked.

On the way down, the girls lost two rosaries. Conchita
lost a rosary belonging to a seminarian and Mari Loli lost

a rosary ring belonging to Father Luis. Our Lady told both of the girls where the rosaries were.

Mari Loli was going to get Father Luis' rosary, but the priest stopped her and said, "Not now; it's late. Tomorrow, in daylight, you can go and find it. If I don't come back again, you keep it safe and give it to my brother when he comes, because he will certainly come."

The next day Mari Loli found the rosary exactly where Our Lady said it would be. Father Luis had already gone so she kept the rosary safe. After the death of his brother, Father Ramon Andreu went to Garabandal as predicted to get the rosary from Mari Loli.

After the vision at the pines, Father Luis joined his friends and traveled down the mountain by jeep to Cosio. There he met Father Valentin.

"Father," said Father Luis, "What the girls say is true, but do not repeat around here what I am telling you now. The Church should use great prudence in these matters."

Father Luis then continued on with his friends, Mr. and Mrs. Fontaneda and their little daughter, Maria Carmen, who was eight years old. Father Luis sat in the front seat next to Jose Salceda, the driver.

They all talked about the events at Garabandal and what it meant.

"How happy I am! I am overflowing with happiness!" exclaimed the priest. "The Virgin Mary gave me such a gift! I do not harbor the slightest doubt about the reality of what has happened to the children! It is the truth!"

It was a long drive and they stopped for some refreshments, but Father Luis only drank a glass of water. He rested for a while and fell asleep for about an hour. When he awoke, he said that he was completely rested and felt very well. It was four o'clock in the morning, and the others were quite tired.

"I am overjoyed!" exclaimed Father Luis again. "I am full of happiness. What a gift the Virgin has given me! How fortunate it is to have a mother in Heaven. We need not fear the supernatural life. We must treat the Virgin as the four children do. They are an example to us. I cannot have the slightest doubt about their vision. Why should the Virgin choose us? This is the happiest day of my life!"

Father Luis became very quiet.

"Father, are you okay? asked Mr. Fontaneda.

The priest bowed his head and gave a little sigh.

Jose, the driver, looked at the priest. "Is he ill?" he asked the others.

Mrs. Fontaneda reached for the priest. He did not move. She felt his pulse. "Stop!" she screamed. "He does not have a pulse. There is a clinic near here."

They rushed to the clinic and rang the doorbell. A nurse came out and hurried to attend to the priest. "He is dead," she declared.

The parish priest was called immediately to administer the sacraments.

Father Luis was only thirty-six years old. He had never been sick except for a slight allergy in the springtime. He never had any type of heart trouble. Everyone talked about what happened. "He died of joy!" they said. "He even had a slight smile on his face when he died."

A few days later, at Garabandal, the four girls had another extraordinary occurrence. During their usual vision they saw a light like they had never seen before. The voice of Father Luis spoke to them. He called them each by name. He told them some things for his brother Ramon, and he taught them some words in French, German and English. He also taught them the Hail Mary in Greek.

Father Luis also sent a message to console his own mother, who had raised four sons to be priests and who was a widow preparing to enter into the Visitation Convent.

"Be happy and content, for I am in Heaven, and I see you every day."

Father Ramon did not believe it when he heard that the

girls were talking with his brother who had died after being in Garabandal. He returned to the village to get the rosary and to observe the girls. The girls told him of events that only the two brothers were aware of which convinced Father Ramon, and he truly believed.

One evening, after she had become a nun, Sister Maria Luisa, Father Luis' mother, was getting ready for bed in her cell. She heard a voice say to her, "Luis is coming."

No one was in the small room, but suddenly the room was illuminated, and Luis was standing there with two other priests. To his mother, Father Luis looked just like he did when he was alive. No words were exchanged between then, because no words were necessary. She knew all that she needed to know. By a special grace from God, this was his final good-bye. They looked at each other and then he left, and the room was again in darkness.

Our Lady told Conchita on July 18, 1964, that Father Luis was in Heaven. She also foretold that on the day after the miracle in the pines, the body of Father Luis would be found incorrupt.

CHAPTER 9

Miracle of the Eucharist

Conchita often said that the Eucharist was the key feature at Garabandal.

From almost the beginning of the apparitions, the four girls asked the Blessed Virgin for a sign or a miracle to convince the people of their visions. Usually Our Lady would simply smile at the girls.

At various times, St. Michael appeared to the girls and would give them Holy Communion. The girls said that at first St. Michael gave them unconsecrated hosts in order to teach them how to receive the Body of Christ with proper respect. Soon he gave them consecrated hosts so that they were able to receive Holy Communion when there was no priest at Garabandal.

In order to prepare for Communion properly, he told the girls to say the prayer "I Confess to God" which is said at the beginning of Mass.

> I confess to almighty God,
> and to you, my brothers and sisters,
> that I have sinned through my own fault,
> in my thoughts and in my words,
> in what I have done,
> and in what I have failed to do;
> and I ask blessed Mary, ever virgin,

all the angels and saints,
and you, my brothers and sisters,
to pray for me to the Lord our God.
May almighty God have mercy on us,
forgive us our sins,
and bring us to everlasting life. Amen.

After Communion, St. Michael told the girls that they should give thanks to God. He taught them the prayer of St. Ignatius Loyola.

Soul of Christ

Soul of Christ, sanctify me.
Body of Christ, save me.
Blood of Christ, inebriate me.
Water from the side of Christ, purify me.
Passion of Christ, fortify me.
O Dear Jesus, hear my prayer.
In your Sacred Wounds, hide me.
Never permit me to stray from You.
From the evil spirit, protect me.
At the hour of my death, call me,
And bid that I come to You.
So that with all Your Saints and
Angels I may praise You
Forever and ever. Amen.

A priest once asked the girls to ask St. Michael where he got the Holy Hosts since only priests can consecrate the bread and wine. The answer was that he took the consecrated Hosts from tabernacles on earth.

When the girls received Holy Communion they could be seen opening their mouths but the Hosts were always invisible to those who were watching. To the girls, however, it was just like receiving Communion at Mass.

On June 22, 1962, during an apparition, St. Michael told Conchita that he would give her Communion and that the Host would be visible. Conchita was surprised because she did not know that the Hosts had been invisible.

Later, Our Lady told Conchita that the date for this miracle would be July 18 and that she could announce it 15 days in advance.

When Conchita made the announcement, the news spread quickly throughout Spain and other parts of Europe. Many people went to Garabandal to see the miracle that was to take place on July 18.

This date was also the special feast day of Saint Sebastian, and the villagers had planned their traditional Mass and celebration. It was a joyous atmosphere but yet solemn. The Mass was followed by music and dancing.

"What if a miracle doesn't happen?" someone asked Conchita.

"Maybe the music and dancing will keep St. Michael away?" someone else said. The loud noise could easily be heard in Conchita's home because she lived close to the party area.

After waiting all day, Conchita's brother, who had grown very restless with the long wait said angrily, "I can't take this any longer. I'm going to bed. It's late. You have badly deceived all of us!" He hurried up the stairs.

"No, don't go. Wait a little longer," Conchita pleaded. She had already had her first calling and was sure the apparition was coming but she did not know when it would be. The dancing finally ended, and many people went home. Those who had come to see the miracle were disappointed, and many of them had gone home too.

Finally at 1:40 a.m., Conchita left her home in ecstasy and went down a lane that had been used as a dumping ground. The people who were waiting for Conchita immediately began to follow her. There was a great deal of pushing and shoving, for everyone wanted to get close to her.

Benjamin Gomez was right next to Conchita. He carefully watched the whole incident.

I saw her kneel down, open her mouth and present her bare tongue. I could see very well, because I was so close, less than the width of my hand from her face. I looked in her mouth, taking my time. I looked up, nothing; I looked down, nothing. At that moment, one of my cousins who was behind me, touched my shoulder so I let him look. I turned my head for one instant. When I looked back the Host was on her tongue.

It was white, but white out of this world. Sometimes I search for a comparison, but I can find only one although very far from reality. We would have said something like snow, a snowflake upon which the sun's rays were striking. But in that case, the white hurts the eyes, whereas the Host did not strain one's eyes.

Pepe Diez, the village mason, was very close to Conchita. He reported the following:

At the moment Conchita fell to her knees, all the people present tried to do the same, some on top of the others; some were able to kneel on the ground, others bowed very profoundly. Everyone was showing great humility. In spite of the mob, everyone was trying to be considerate of their neighbor which was not easy.

But I did not take my eyes off the girl. She started to speak, to pray, and then she smiled, and while smiling, she opened her mouth and put out her tongue very naturally. I had a terrible feeling of disaster, for in my naivete, I had thought that at the precise moment Conchita put out her tongue we would see the Host, or that the Host would appear instantaneously, or who knows what?

I was scarcely 18 inches away from her face and the sight of her bare tongue gave me a terrible feeling of failure. I was hoping for so much!

Conchita kept her tongue out like that for about a minute. And as I stood there, my eyes riveted on her, something incredible happened! Without moving my eyes for a fraction of a second, suddenly a neat, precise and well-formed Host appeared miraculously on Conchita's tongue. I can attest to the fact that from the moment Conchita put out her tongue, she did not make a single move, either with her mouth or with her tongue; not a single muscle in her face moved.

Her tongue was out and bare, and then all of a sudden the Host was there! I did not see how it came. It was instantaneous! I can't even say it arrived in a split second. It was just there! This is what I call the most significant part of the miracle.

This miracle of the Eucharist was extremely significant for it showed the truly miraculous nature of the Blessed Sacrament, which is the great miracle that is performed in every Mass throughout the world. At Garabandal Our Lady was truly bringing her Son to us in the most miraculous manner.

Many people were disappointed with the miracle of the Eucharist. They had gone to Garabandal for the miracle that was to be on July 18. They had waited throughout the entire day, and it was not until 1:40 a.m. on July 19 that the miracle actually occurred. For some, running through the rocky streets at night and falling to ones knees and receiving Holy Communion from an angel was just a bit too much.

People pushed and shoved to see the miracle, but the streets were too narrow and crowded so only the people who were very close to Conchita actually saw the Host on her tongue.

What was thought to be an act to help convince the people that the apparitions were actually occurring turned out to be nothing of the kind. People were simply relying

on the testimony of those near the child, and most of
those people were villagers who already believed anyway.

Alejandro Damians was a businessman from Barcelona,
Spain. He had heard about the events at Garabandal and
decided to go there. He borrowed a friend's movie camera
and was going to try to film whatever he saw.

> There was a great deal of confusion. Because
> I am tall, the people behind me kept saying,
> "Get down!" and then someone hit me in the
> head with something. I crouched over and Con-
> chita was on her knees. I took the camera out
> of the bag and looked through the lens without
> making any adjustments or anything. I made
> sure I could see Conchita's head and shot. I
> caught the last seconds of the miracle.

It was true. The pictures that Mr. Damians took that
night with his borrowed movie camera showed the visible
host appear on Conchita's tongue. This was the evidence
that so many people were looking for. The pictures circu-
lated as more and more people believed the girls.

Mr. Damians himself experienced a very emotional encounter that night, which he explained to a Dr. Caux who
was also in Garabandal on July 18 to photograph the
event.

"Did you feel at that moment a joy so immense, so
far out of this world, that you couldn't share it with anyone and that you wouldn't exchange for anything in this
world?" asked Dr. Caux, explaining by the question some
of his own feelings.

"I would not exchange the bliss which I felt in those
moments for anything in the world. It was a joy, deep
and intense, which I cannot explain nor share with anyone. Something utterly different from the ordinary; something for which I would give my life, and which did not
permit me afterward to follow the young girl in ecstasy,
nor my wife nor anyone, but forced me to go into a corner

and weep in silence," answered Mr. Damians.

"There are two things I would like to know: Why was your joy so profound; and, if I may ask, were you in a state of grace that day?" asked Dr. Caux.

"I was in the grace of God. I am going to tell you something great; my impression of what I saw was of meeting the true God. Therefore, I would not exchange it for anything in the world. If God wants me to see the Miracle, I will be delighted. But if not, I don't believe anything in the world could produce in me a deeper impression than the one I had of having seen Him in that solemn and greatest moment of my life," answered Mr. Damians.

"Let me tell you," replied Dr. Caux. "You make me happy on one hand and sad on the other. I felt the same thing but only in reverse. I had prepared everything to film the event and was more ready than ever. But it all went wrong, and I could not film at all. I had permission from the Bishop and also Conchita, but for some reason unknown to me, I was not able to get permission from the pastor. It was only at the last moment, at the last fraction of a second, that I was able to see the Host which disappeared, swallowed by the girl. At that moment I felt a dreadful, inexplicable sorrow which choked me because I could but catch a glimpse of God as He fled from me. It was at that moment I thought that I was in the state of mortal sin. I also wept, but out of sorrow, because at that moment I understood what Hell and sin were, because I saw no hope of relief for my sorrow and feeling of disgrace. My wife wanted to comfort me, but I could not explain. Anyway, she could not have understood. It was a sorrow too great to be shared or consoled, and I believe that only if God allows me to see the Miracle, and I remain by Him in His grace, will this sorrow leave me. This sorrow was so deep that I believe it would have killed me. It still pierces my heart. I could not join the crowd which shouted with enthusiasm 'The Host! The Host!' I was deprived of this joy and of what they had seen, except at the last moment. I also felt that the villagers avoided me; I thought they saw my sin. I know now what God is and what He wants of me. I know the hell of not seeing God and how this pain was relieved through confession. Believe me, the sight of Hell moves me to the point of causing me to move the world, announcing to it the coming Miracle in order that it may be saved. I anxiously work toward that event as if I were the only one to know of it.''

Dr. Caux later remembered an event that happened that night which was very important. After the miracle of the Host, Conchita, still in ecstasy, walking backward, approached him, and with her back to him, gave him the crucifix she was carrying to kiss three times. Dr. Caux truly believed that this act showed the mercy of God.

Everything that happened that night was so significant and parallels the teachings of the Church.

First, Conchita had gone to Mass and Holy Communion in the morning of July 18. Church law at that time did not permit one to receive Holy Communion more than once a day. St. Michael complied with the Church law and waited until after midnight to give Conchita the Blessed Host.

Also, since he did not have permission from the parish priest to film the event, Dr. Caux, out of obedience and respect for the Church did not film Conchita while she was receiving the Host.

The description of the feeling of the two men are incredible, as they truly show good and evil and the mercy of God.

Respect for the Holy Eucharist was one of the main concerns of Our Lady, and she was teaching this respect through the children.

CHAPTER 10

The Authorities

Father Valentin Marichalar was the pastor of the church of San Sebastian. He was also the pastor for the church in Cosio, where he lived. He was a kind and gentle man who enjoyed going to Garabandal and saying the Sunday Mass for the people. He knew the villagers because he was the one who baptized the babies, married the couples and buried the dead.

He made a special trip back up the mountain, when he first heard about the apparitions, to interview the girls. He was very impressed with the statements the girls made, and after he saw them in ecstasy, he knew that he must notify the Bishop of Santandar.

As soon as the Bishop was notified about the apparitions, he sent another priest to the village to evaluate the situation. Doctors were also sent to Garabandal immediately to test the girls.

Since Conchita seemed to be the most intelligent of the girls and was definitely the leader, the priests decided that she should go to Santandar to speak with the Bishop. In this way they could observe the three other little girls and see if they continued with the unusual behavior without Conchita.

Priests and doctors continually interrogated Conchita while she was in Santandar. They tried to convince her that she was wrong and that she had not seen any visions.

Our Lady appeared to Conchita one day in Santandar, which brought the little girl great joy. Conchita's ecstasy was at the same time as the other girls in Garabandal.

Our Lady told Mari Loli, Mari Cruz and Jacinta that Conchita was in ecstasy at the same time that they were.

"How lovely," responded the girls. "Conchita is seeing you, too!"

Conchita went into a trance in front of the Church of La Consolacion. This was by no means a coincidence, for Our Lady was truly consoling the small child who had suffered a great deal, being away from her home, family, friends and not having the usual apparitions.

Our Lady told Conchita that she would not be having apparitions in Santandar because she would be going to the beach. She said that the other girls would continue to have apparitions.

As it turned out, the doctors and priests decided that all Conchita needed was to play with other girls her age and go to the beach. She was taken to the beach every day. They thought that these simple distractions would make the child forget all about the apparitions.

After a week, Conchita's mother decided that it was time to get her child. She went to Santandar, and against the doctors and priests wishes, she brought her little girl home.

Conchita told the doctors that she had not seen the Virgin but that the other girls had. She meant that she was not seeing the Virgin while she was in Santandar. She wanted to go home so that she too could once again see the Virgin Mary. The doctors took her statement as a denial of ever seeing the apparition, which, of course, was completely wrong.

When Conchita and her mother arrived back at Garabandal, they were suprised to see several priests and visitors hurrying out to meet them.

"How did you know that we were coming?" asked Conchita's mother.

"Mari Loli and Jacinta are in the church," answered a priest. "They just announced that Our Lady said that Conchita was coming up the road. We came out to see if it were true."

More priests, doctors and other church officials came to Garabandal to interview the girls and watch them during an ecstasy. Many tried to disprove the happening by mocking the "running around" that the girls did and also by saying that there were too many apparitions. At Lourdes, Bernadette had only received 18 apparitions and the three children at Fatima, only six.

A commission was established to study the events at Garabandal. The commission declared that it was too early to make any judgments concerning the nature of the phenomena, but they could not say that there was anything supernatural occurring. The commission did not interview the adults in Garabandal who were witnesses to what was happening, including Father Valentin Marichalar, the pastor who had kept perfect records of the events from the beginning.

The commission recommended that priests and members of the clergy should abstain from going to San Sebastian de Garabandal until the ecclesiastical authorities passed final judgment. The faithful were advised not to go to the village.

On October 27, 1961, Bishop Cirarda of Santandar also sent out a formal letter stating that it would be wise to forestall any hasty or imprudent interpretations until the Church passes final judgment on the events at Garabandal.

He told priests to refrain from anything that might contribute to creating confusion among the faithful. He also reminded them that everything that the Church teaches has already been revealed and that we do not need to support unproven revelations and miracles.

"If He, Himself or through His Blessed Mother, thinks fit to speak to us, we should be attentive to hear His words and say to Him like Samuel: 'Speak on, Lord, Thy servant is listening!'" He ended by declaring, "Final judgment remains subject to the events that may take place in the future."

At the end of 1962, Father Valentin Marichalar was replaced as the pastor of Cosio because of his belief in the apparitions. The new priest was ordered to be extremely prudent.

Father Amador Gonzalez, the new priest, had his orders, and the girls were not allowed to enter the church for any more apparitions. Our Lady would lead them to the church or they would walk around the church, but after the priest refused to permit the girls inside they never had an apparition inside the church again. St. Michael would sometimes give them Holy Communion in front of the church, but he too was obedient to the church order.

Many restrictions were imposed upon the girls, but the apparitions apparently continued to occur, and the people continued to go to Garabandal. Conversions were observed, healings were reported and an aura of deep spirituality was felt at Garabandal.

The main confusion began when the girls had their own doubts. They were tormented with feelings of remorse and despair. They began to contradict each other and deny that they had seen the visions, just as Our Lady had foretold earlier. The girls went through many trials during this time. Our Lady had explained to the girls that they would establish among themselves the same confusion that now exists in the Church.

A priest who was studying the events at Garabandal immediately protested when he heard this statement, for he said, "It can't be the Blessed Virgin who is appearing, for there isn't any confusion in the Church. It must be of the devil."

Since that time, however, there has been a great deal of confusion in the Church concerning many matters, but in 1961 such a thing seemed impossible.

On October 7, 1962, Bishop Aldazabal wrote, "We prohibit all priests, whether of the diocese or not, and all religious from gathering at the aforementioned site (Garabandal) without express permission from the diocesan authorities."

On November 29, 1962, Conchita wrote to Fr. Jose Ramon Garcia de la Riva and said that the Bishop would say that all who wish may come on the day of the miracle. On December 5, 1962, she said that the Bishop of Santandar would lift the restrictions shortly before the Miracle.

On July 8, 1965, Bishop Beitia wrote:

> "...We have found no grounds for an ecclesiastical condemnation either in the doctrine or in the spiritual recommendations that have been divulged in the events and addressed to the Christian faithful. Furthermore, these recommendations contain exhortations to prayer, sacrifice, devotion to the Holy Eucharist and devotion to the Blessed Virgin under traditional praiseworthy forms; these are also exhortations to a holy fear of the Lord offended by our sins..."

Although Santander claimed that there was nothing supernatural in the events at Garabandal, Rome had other feelings. In 1966, Conchita was summoned to Rome so that she could be personally interviewed by the Sacred Congregation of the Doctrine of Faith. She met Pope Paul VI and also Padre Pio.

In 1966, as a result of the Vatican Council, the Holy See abolished Canon Laws 1399 and 2318 which dealt with private revelations. This made it possible to visit places of alleged apparitions, like Garabandal, provided faith and morals were not jeopardized.

In 1975, Jacinta also went to Rome and was greeted favorably by many of the Bishops and Cardinals. She answered questions for officials in the Sacred Congregation of Faith and impressed them all with her simplicity and dignity. They agreed with her request to let the visiting priests say Mass, adding that it was up to the Bishop of Santandar to fulfill the request.

In 1986, Bishop Juan Antonio del Val Gallo instituted a new investigation of the apparitions at Garabandal. That fall he went to Rome and submitted documentation to The Sacred Congregation for the Doctrine of the Faith on the apparitions.

Bishop del Val said that he did not see any inconvenience, as far as he was concerned, in having a pontifical commission for the Holy See examine these phenomena with the collaboration of the diocese of Santandar.

In January of 1987, in time for the Marian Year, the Bishop issued a new directive where priests who visit Garabandal were free to celebrate Mass on their own in the village church, removing the restrictions that were imposed in 1962.

In 1965, Conchita said that before the Warning, there would be a pre-warning. "At the Episcopal See of Santander, there will come a bishop who will not believe in the events at first; but the Blessed Virgin will give him a sign. He will then believe and will lift the prohibition for the priests to go to Garabandal." The Warning will be very close to that time.

Since 1961 there have been six bishops of Santandar. The first two bishops issued notes of caution, which was quite natural in such cases. The second bishop, however, did pronounce the messages to be in perfect keeping with the tenets of the Church.

Both the third and fourth bishops denied the supernatural character of the phenomena. The fifth bishop doubted the apparitions at first but has become quite favorable toward them, lifting the prohibition of the priests and allowing them to say Mass.

The new bishop, Jose Vilaplana Blasco, became Bishop

of Santandar September 29, 1991, on the feast day of St. Michael. This may be a significant feature and of important relevance to Garabandal. It was soon realized that this bishop did not believe in the events at first. On October 11, 1996, he released a statement concluding that he did not find it necessary to have a new public declaration about Garabandal but that he agreed with his predecessors, all the bishops of Santandar since 1961, and found no evidence of supernatural validity of the apparitions. He did not condemn the apparitions but simply stated he found no evidence of supernatural validity.

"I agree with [and] I accept the decision of my predecessors and the direction of the Holy See," he wrote. "In reference to the Eucharistic celebration in Garabandal, following the decision of my predecessors, I ruled that Masses can be celebrated only in the parish church and there will be no references to the alleged apparitions and visiting priests who want to say Mass must have approval from the pastor, who has my authorization. It is my wish that this information is helpful to you."

The Bishop wrote the statement in response to the many inquiries he had received about the events at Garabandal. He explained to the visionaries that he had neither forbidden the belief in the apparitions nor had he implied that people should not go to Garabandal in pilgrimage. He put the restriction on visiting priests to only celebrate Mass in the parish church out of respect for the Holy Eucharist. He was aware of the fact that some Masses had been said in the pine area and other apparition sites and he wanted to discourage this practice. By saying they should say Mass in the Church, he was implying that they have his permission to go to Garabandal to pray.

CHAPTER 11

Sacraments and Sacramentals

The seven Sacraments are visible signs instituted by Jesus Christ, by which the graces of the Holy Spirit are communicated to us. Through these Sacraments we may gain Eternal Salvation.

Sacramentals are those rites, actions and things which the Church uses in imitation of the Sacraments for a spiritual nature. A sacramental produces grace indirectly. The most common sacramentals are prayers, holy water, blessed candles, vestments, rosaries, medals, crucifixes and scapulars.

At Garabandal, the Blessed Virgin Mary taught the importance of the Sacraments and sacramentals of the Church. Through her actions and messages she shows how the Sacraments can lead us to eternal happiness with God.

BAPTISM

By Baptism we are made Christians, children of God, members of His holy Church and heirs of Heaven. The people of Garabandal had very little material goods, but they were wealthy in their spirituality. They valued their Baptisms and took their Baptismal vows faithfully.

On March 31, 1962, Mari Loli's mother had a baby girl. Mari Loli was not in the room, but she went into ecstasy shortly after the baby was born.

"Oh! It is a little sister!" she exclaimed. "What, so little, and sin already in her?"

Our Lady explained to Mari Loli about Original Sin and how Baptism is necessary to wash away the sin. Of course, the parents had their new daughter, Guadelupe, baptized as soon as possible.

Another incident happened concerning Baptism when two young women went to Garabandal. Catherine was an eighteen-year-old from Paris, and her friend Ascension (Chon) de Luis was from Burgos, Spain. Catherine was not a Catholic, but she was very interested in the Catholic religion. She was staying with her friend, Chon, to study Spanish. While visiting with Chon, Catherine had gone to Mass and had learned to say the rosary.

When she returned home she asked her parents if she could become a Catholic. Her parents discouraged it, but told her that she could do whatever she wanted when she became twenty-one years old.

Catherine returned to Spain to continue her studies. One day she and Chon went into a store to find a little cross. There they learned about the apparitions at Garabandal. The girls decided to see for themselves what was happening.

As in so many apparitions of our Holy Mother, a priest had mentioned that maybe the apparition was from the devil and suggested to Jacinta and Mari Loli that they bring holy water with them to sprinkle at the vision.

Thus, Catherine and Chon prepared a small bottle of holy water and waited for the vision at Jacinta's home with eight or nine other people. Both girls, their parents and Father Valentin were present along with the two young women, Catherine and Chon.

Soon Jacinta and Mari Loli went into ecstasy. They explained how the priest had said the vision might be from the devil, and with expressions of sadness and fear, they could be heard telling Our Lady that they were going to use the holy water to chase the devils away. Immediately their expressions changed from fear to joy and the two little girls smiled radiantly.

Their conversation could be heard by all those in the room. "She isn't a Catholic?...She isn't baptized?... Come...Help her?...Oh! Because of her parents..." The conversation continued.

Finally Jacinta and Mari Loli began to offer Our Lady the objects to be kissed. Mari Loli handed a rosary that belonged to Chon.

"Oh, with this rosary she learned to pray. She said her first Hail Mary with this rosary!" said Mari Loli, repeating the words of the vision.

Chon was amazed because it was true. She had taught Catherine how to say the prayers. It was her rosary that Mari Loli was holding. No one else could have known.

Jacinta then picked up the rosary, which Mari Loli had placed on her lap with the other objects, and again offered it to be kissed. "Her first Hail Mary!" said Jacinta.

Chon's rosary was kissed twice by Our Lady. She later learned that it was the only object that Our Lady had ever accepted to kiss twice.

Then Loli said, "Now?...Good!" and reached for the little bottle of holy water. She threw its contents upward toward the vision.

To the shock of everyone in the room, the water did not follow a normal course. It made an impossible curve, hung in the air for a moment and then the water fell all over Catherine! Not a drop of water fell on anyone else, even those who were close to the young women.

On October 20, 1963, Catherine was officially baptized in the Cathedral at Burgos. She chose the name "Maria del Carmen" for her baptismal name at the suggestion of Conchita. Many of their friends from Garabandal attended the ceremony performed by Fr. Ramon Andreu, brother of the late Fr. Luis Andreu.

PENANCE

Penance is the Sacrament by which the sins committed after Baptism are forgiven, whereby we are reconciled with God, mankind and ourselves. This Sacrament (also known as Confession) prepares us for Holy Communion so that our souls will be clean when we receive Jesus Christ.

Jacinta said that the Blessed Virgin spoke with them about the Sacrament of Penance. She said that it was very important to recognize within ourselves that we have sinned, and to make an effort not to sin again. In this way we are able to improve ourselves.

Mari Cruz asked St. Michael to hear her confession. He answered that he did not have that power. Our Lady also said that she did not have the power to forgive sins.

One day, Conchita, Mari Loli and Jacinta were in ecstasy, kneeling to receive the Host from St. Michael. Both Conchita and Mari Loli received the Host, but St. Michael did not offer it to Jacinta.

Jacinta was very upset, but St. Michael explained that it was because she had argued with her mother and had been disrespectful and that she must go to Confession before she received Holy Communion.

One day a priest asked the girls to ask Our Lady what the people should do to amend their lives.

"They should confess and receive the Eucharist," the Blessed Virgin replied on September 8, 1961.

Again on October 7, 1962, on the feast of Our Lady of the Rosary, after Mari Loli asked what people should do, Our Lady said, *"Confess and receive Communion."*

Almost the entire village of Garabandal went to Confession after the night when the girls had the terrible vision of the chastisement and were heard screaming.

Our Lady told the girls about the horror of sin and the consequence of sin. Conchita echoed the words of our last three popes when she said, "We have lost the sense of sin." But in spite of this, Our Lady also teaches about the mercy of God. *"If you ask His forgiveness with sincere hearts, He will pardon you."*

The Blessed Virgin taught the girls to avoid and dread sin.

HOLY COMMUNION

Holy Communion is the Body, Blood, Soul and Divinity of Our Lord Jesus Christ, under the appearances of bread and wine. It is the food of our souls. It is a Sacrament. It is also the Sacrifice of the Mass in which He is offered up for us to His Eternal Father.

At Garabandal, the Holy Eucharist is the focal point. The famous sign and miracle of Garabandal was when the Holy Host was seen on Conchita's tongue.

The importance of the Holy Eucharist was stressed over and over again when Our Lady would tell the people to *confess and receive Communion.*

She asked for frequent visits to her Son in the Blessed Sacrament. During her last message to Conchita, Our Lady said, *"You must visit the Blessed Sacrament frequently. Less and less importance is being given to the Eucharist. Why do you not go more often to visit my Son in the tabernacle? He waits for you there, day and night."* Saying the rosary in the presence of the Blessed Sacrament does much to add to our graces.

The people all commented on the reverence with which Father Luis Andreu received Communion during his last Mass. Many said, after the Mass, that he looked like a saint. Everyone talked about the holiness of the priest, and after his death, he became the saint of Garabandal. Our Lady had told the girls that Father Luis was in Heaven.

When a priest asked the girls where St. Michael got the Hosts to give them, they answered that he took the consecrated Hosts out of the tabernacles of the world.

They were then asked which was greater, the angel or the priest? Conchita replied that the priest had more power than the angel, for only he can say Mass and consecrate hosts.

Our Lady said that it was a greater grace to receive Jesus in Holy Communion than to see her.

The main emphasis, as given by Our Lady at Garabandal, is devotion to the Blessed Sacrament and prayers for priests.

Jacinta's father noticed that the children showed an enormous respect for the Holy Eucharist while they were in church. When the girls were in the church in ecstasy, they always walked backward from the altar and the tabernacle until they reached the door. "Never in ecstasy did they turn their backs to the Blessed Sacrament. Never! In reality, their manner of acting was a lesson for us."

Our Lady warned that the number of people who would make visits to the Blessed Sacrament would decline and that there would also be a loss of respect toward the Blessed Sacrament.

"Be careful, I am warning you in advance, the time is soon coming when people will rarely visit the Blessed Sacrament and when many will fail to maintain a respectful attitude in its presence," said Our Lady.

Conchita said that indifference to the Blessed Sacrament was a great offense to Our Lord. When people walk into the church talking and being disrespectful, they are being very offensive. Their appearance and attitude is often irreverent, and people must stop and realize where they are and who they are visiting. The true belief in the Real Presence of Christ is essential for proper devotion.

HOLY ORDERS

Our Lady often talked with the girls about priests, for she loved them and said that they were "her chosen sons." During a conversation that was taped, one of the girls was describing a man she had seen and she thought that he was a priest.

"He was wearing a white habit and shoes with holes

in the top," she said as she described the clothing and sandals.

It was obvious that Our Lady told the girls that the priest was a Dominican because after a brief pause the child could be heard to say, "Oh, yes, a Dominican." The girls did not know about the various religious orders and were surprised by the different priests who went to Garabandal.

In almost every apparition, Our Lady asked the children of Garabandal to pray for priests. The priest's primary role is a minister of the Eucharist, and Our Lady's concern for these ministers was very evident. She asked us to pray for priests because the faithful follow their example.

In her message on June 18, 1965, the Blessed Virgin told Conchita, *"Many cardinals, bishops and priests are on the road to perdition and are taking many souls with them."* This was an extremely disturbing message, and many people felt that no one would ever speak of the clergy in such harsh terms.

Since 1965, however, there has been much turmoil within the Church, and with all of the changes and new ideas, many priests and nuns have deserted their holy vows. Through improper counsel and example, many souls have indeed been led astray. In retrospect, Our Lady's words are easy to understand, but at the time the message was given, it was very hard to comprehend.

On July 20, 1963, Our Lord said to Conchita during a locution:

> *Concerning priests, pray much for them so that they may be holy and fulfill their duty properly and make others better. May they make me known to those who ignore me, and may they make me loved by those who know but do not love me.*

Our Lady showed her special love for priests by teaching the children to know and recognize priests and to obey them. Even when a priest would go to Garabandal wearing the clothing of a lay person, the girls would recognize him as a priest.

The girls loved the priests very much and prayed for them constantly. When a new priest would enter the village the girls would find him and talk with him. Every priest was considered an important visitor.

Conchita wrote a letter to a French priest in answer to his question of what the Blessed Virgin wants of a priest.

> What the Blessed Virgin wants of the priest is, first of all, his own sanctification. He should fulfill his vows through love of God. To lead many souls to God in any other way is difficult in our day.
>
> May he be saintly, for love of souls in Christ. May he occasionally seclude himself in silence to listen to God who speaks to him continually.
>
> May he think frequently about the passion of Jesus so that his life may be more united to Christ the Priest. Thus, he will lead souls to penance and sacrifice and will help them to better carry the cross that Jesus asks all of us to carry.
>
> He should speak of Mary who is the one who will most surely lead us to Christ. He should also speak to souls and make them believe that as there is a Heaven, so too, there is a Hell.
>
> I believe that is what Heaven wants of its priests.

Father Luis Andreu was an excellent example of how a holy priest should act. And he was rewarded by seeing the miracle.

Padre Pio was another of Our Lady's chosen sons who was privileged to see the miracle before he died.

In January of 1966, Conchita visited Padre Pio after having received a letter from him saying, "They do not believe in you or in your conversations with the Lady in white, but they will believe when it will be too late."

During her visit, Padre Pio blessed a crucifix that Our Lady had kissed for Conchita. He also blessed a rosary that Our Lady had kissed, for Conchita's mother. These two sacramentals became doubly blessed.

One of the prophecies that Our Lady made at Garabandal was that Padre Pio would see the miracle, too. Conchita was very upset to hear of Padre Pio's death on September 23, 1968. Not only was her good friend dead, but she thought that the prediction of him seeing the miracle was then impossible.

On October 16, 1968, Conchita received a telegram asking her to meet with Padre Pio's emissaries at Lourdes. Conchita and her mother went to Lourdes and met Fr. Cennamo and Fr. Pellegrino.

The two priests gave Conchita a letter from Padre Pio and the veil that covered his face when he was in his coffin. Before he died, he requested that "Conchita from Garabandal" be given the veil.

"How is it that the Virgin told me Padre Pio was supposed to see the miracle, and now he is dead?" Conchita asked the priests.

"He saw the miracle before he died," Father Cennamo assured her. "He told me so himself."

In the note from Padre Pio, Conchita read, "I pray to the Most Holy Virgin to comfort you and guide you always toward sanctity, and I bless you with all my heart."

CONFIRMATION

Confirmation is the Sacrament by which we receive the Holy Spirit to make us strong and holy Christians and soldiers of Jesus Christ.

The gifts of the Holy Spirit are: wisdom, knowledge, understanding, fortitude, piety, prudence and fear of the Lord. These gifts can easily be seen reflected in the visionaries and the villagers of Garabandal.

The girls were also models for certain virtues which Our Lady taught them. She told them the value of obedience to their parents and to the Church. She told them to be modest in their dress and even had them change their clothes when they were once dressed inappropriately. They were taught humility, and each girl became an example of humility. They were meek and humble and never proud that they were the chosen ones of Our Lady.

"What God loves above all is humility; what displeases Him above all is pride," Our Lady told the girls. *"Love humility, simplicity. Never think that what you have done is much."*

The Holy Spirit guided the girls and their parents to make the right decisions during their lives. Conchita and Jacinta both prayed for the vocation to become a nun, but they were denied this great privilege. Through the Holy Spirit they were led to understand their true vocations and how they were supposed to do the will of God.

The girls all displayed an unusual amount of peace and joy in their lives. They said that the Blessed Virgin smiled a lot, and they too smiled and appeared to be very happy. While in ecstasy, the girls' faces were transformed and reflected a "heavenly peace and an overflowing joy."

The fruit of the Spirit is charity, joy, peace (*Gal.* 5:22).

The girls' display of charity was always evident. They helped their families and neighbors. In Garabandal, everyone always helped each other, thereby transforming the entire village into a good example of what charity is all about.

MATRIMONY

From the very beginnings of the apparitions at Garabandal, Our Blessed Mother showed her love for the Holy Sacrament of Matrimony by kissing blessed wedding rings.

The wedding ring is an important symbol of everlasting unity and is a sacramental sign of the union of husband and wife.

Conchita's Aunt Maximina was visiting her one day while Jacinta was in ecstasy.

"This wedding ring is blessed," said Maximina. "See if the Virgin will kiss it." She handed Conchita the ring.

Conchita then moved close to Jacinta and said, "Take this ring and give it to the Virgin."

Jacinta was heard saying, "Take the ring! Kiss it! Oh! It's Maximina's!" She then went to Maximina, while still in ecstasy, and put the ring on the correct finger.

There was no way that Jacinta could have known that the ring was Maximina's except that the Blessed Virgin told her.

Another time someone gave Mari Loli ten wedding rings to be kissed. After Our Lady kissed the rings, Mari Loli returned them to their rightful owners and put them on the correct finger of each person. One lady was a widow and received two rings, her own and her husband's.

Once the girls asked the Blessed Virgin what parental sin offended her the most. Our Lady replied that the family quarreling that went on between parents sorrowed her the most. The harmony intended for marriage was destroyed by unnecessary argument and contention. She wanted to establish unity of heart and mind in marriage.

In order to show the importance of marriage and the family, Our Lady appeared to the visionaries in the home of each family of Garabandal at one time or another.

Each family accepted these "visitations" with humility and reverence to think that the Mother of their God should visit in their home.

All four of the visionaries eventually married and have good solid Catholic homes where they live in love and harmony and teach their children to love God and His Holy Mother. Family prayers are a very important part of their daily lives.

Through the lives of the visionaries, Our Lady has stressed the importance of the Holy Sacrament of Matrimony. Some people have tried to dishonor this holy state, but at Garabandal Our Lady elevated it to the position given by God.

ANOINTING OF THE SICK

Anointing of the sick is the Sacrament which, through prayers and the anointing with oil, is conferred on those who are seriously ill or in danger of death. This sacrament can be made conditionally if there is doubt of life.

In the case of Father Luis Andreu, who apparently died instantly, a priest and a doctor were both called as soon as possible. The priest arrived first and anointed his fellow priest. This act showed the value placed upon this holy Sacrament.

Many times while the four girls were in ecstasy they would go to homes of sick people in the village and present the crucifix to be kissed. The girls would fall to their knees and pray at the bedside of the sick person.

To pray for the sick, the dying and even those who were dead was a very important part of the prayer life in Garabandal. They had the time honored practice of having a person go through the village each evening at twilight to ring a bell to remind the people to pray for the poor souls.

Father Valentin, the pastor at Garabandal, said that during the twenty years he was in charge of the parish, he never knew of anyone who died in Garabandal without receiving the Sacraments.

After the apparitions were over, Dr. Morales, a Catholic psychiatrist and member of the Commission, was in a state of emotional agitation. His wife was in the hospital with terminal cancer, and although she had been a good practicing Catholic early in their marriage, she had become very negative about God and the Church and had even sent a priest away from her deathbed.

She was suffering very much and did not have long to live. Dr. Morales could find no peace since his wife was dying without the value of the Sacraments, but no matter what he did she would refuse his requests.

There was a man in the hospital who was suffering from the same terminal cancer, and Dr. Morales would talk with him each day. He noticed that the man always clasped a crucifix in his hands, and finally the doctor asked about it.

"My friend, Maria Herroro, brought the crucifix to me and said that it had been kissed by Our Lady at Garabandal, and she would cure me," said Antonio Cavero. "I believe I will be cured."

"Please, share the crucifix with my wife," begged Dr. Morales. "She is dying and she needs a priest, but she won't allow one into her room."

After much pleading, a deal was worked out between the two men. Antonio would hold the crucifix during the day and Mrs. Morales would hold it during the night.

Dr. Morales explained the story to his wife and she willingly accepted the crucifix. Her pain decreased and she found peace in her heart. Soon she asked to receive the last Sacraments, and the family friend, Bishop del Val, came and administered the Sacrament of the Sick to her. She died in peace, and her husband's prayers were answered.

Antonio, on the other hand, became much worse. He was sent to the intensive care unit, and the family was told that he would not live. He too received the last Sacraments on the thirtieth of December.

On January 1, the doctor rushed into Antonio's room. "I don't believe in God, but what is happening to Antonio is a miracle!" he exclaimed. They had run the tests over and over again and found that Antonio had been cured. Antonio went home and was back to work a few weeks later.

Dr. Morales was amazed by the two miracles that he

had witnessed due to the crucifix kissed by Our Lady. Since that time he has become a worker for Our Lady of Garabandal and has spread her message to everyone he meets.

CHAPTER 12

The Last Apparition

Conchita received her last apparition at the pines of Garabandal on November 13, 1965. Our Lady had previously asked her to bring religious objects to be kissed, for they would have great value.

Conchita felt an unusually strong longing to see the Blessed Virgin Mary and the Infant Jesus. She hurried to the pines in spite of the pouring rain.

As she walked, Conchita became overcome with sorrow for her faults and felt a true sense of repentance. She resolved to stay away from sin and to keep her soul pure for God. She felt that she was unworthy to meet the Mother of God and must beg pardon for her sins.

"I heard a very sweet voice, clearly that of the Blessed Virgin, which is easily distinguishable from all others, calling me by name," Conchita later said.

"What do you want?" she answered.

Conchita looked up and saw the beautiful Blessed Virgin with the Infant Jesus in her arms.

"I have brought you rosary beads to kiss!" exclaimed the young girl.

"So I see," was the gentle reply.

Conchita had a piece of chewing gum in her mouth. When the apparition began, she stuck the gum up on a tooth.

Our Lady, knowing about the gum said, *"Why don't you get rid of your chewing gum and offer it up as a sacrifice for the glory of my Son?"*

Ashamed, Conchita took the gum out of her mouth and threw it on the ground.

"You will recall what I told you on your patronal feast day (December 8—Feast of the Immaculate Conception), *that you would suffer much on earth? Well, have confidence in us, and offer your suffering generously to our Hearts for the welfare of your brethren. In this way, you will feel how close we are to you."*

Conchita replied, "How unworthy I am, dear Mother, of the numerous graces I have received through you. And yet, you come to me today to lighten the little cross that I now carry."

Our Blessed Mother then reminded her, *"Conchita, I have not come for your sake alone. I have come for all my children, so that I may draw them closer to our Hearts. Give me everything you have brought so that I may kiss it."*

Our Lady kissed the objects. She also kissed a crucifix that Conchita had and said, *"Place it in the hands of the Infant Jesus."*

Conchita placed the crucifix in the hands of the Infant in Our Lady's arms. He put His hands on the crucifix, but He did not say a word.

"This cross," asked Conchita, "will I take it to the convent with me?"

Our Lady did not reply. She only looked at Conchita.

Finally Our Lady said, *"Through the kiss I have bestowed on these objects, my Son will perform prodigies. Distribute them to others."*

"I will be glad to do this," said Conchita.

Our Lady asked about personal petitions of some of the people. Conchita made the requests that had been given to her.

"Talk to me, Conchita, talk to me about my children.

I hold them all beneath my mantle," whispered Our Loving Mother.

"It is very small, we can't all get under it," replied Conchita.

She said Our Lady smiled and then said, *"Do you know, Conchita, why I did not come myself on June 18, to deliver the message for the world? Because it saddened me to tell it to you myself. But I have to tell you it for your own good, and if you all fulfill it, for the Glory of God. I love you all very much, and I desire your salvation and to gather you all here in Heaven with the Father, the Son and the Holy Spirit. We can count on you, Conchita, can we not?"*

"If I were to see you continually, I would say 'yes'. But, if not, I don't know, because I am so bad," answered the girl as truthfully as possible.

"You do everything that you can, and we will help you," promised Our Lady. *"This will be the last time you see me here. But I shall always be with you and with all my children."*

Later Our Lady said, *"Conchita, why do you not go more often to visit my Son in the tabernacle? He waits for you there, day and night."*

"I am so happy when I see both of you. Why don't you take me now to Heaven with you?" said Conchita as she gazed at Our Lady and Child.

"Remember what I told you," was her Motherly reply. *"When you present yourself before God, your hands must be filled with good works done for your brothers and for the Glory of God. But at the present time, your hands are empty."*

Conchita wrote these words in her diary so that she would have an exact record of the conversation. She said that the joyous time had passed in which she was with her best friend and Mother in Heaven and with the Child Jesus. She had stopped seeing them, but she hasn't stopped feeling them for they will be with her always. Her soul was full of peace, joy and a desire to overcome her faults. She loved the Hearts of Jesus and Mary with all her strength and knows that they love her.

CHAPTER 13

The Visionaries

CONCHITA

Conchita was twelve years old when the apparitions began. She was a pretty girl with brown eyes and long brown hair. Her mother, Aniceta, was a widow. Conchita had three older brothers, Serafin, Aniceto and Miguel.

They lived in a poor, small home at the far side of the village. They were a very religious family, as were most of the families in Garabandal. Each evening, after the meal, they said the family rosary. They would all go to Mass and Communion whenever a priest celebrated Mass in the village. Often, Aniceta would walk the four miles to Cosio for the 6 a.m. Mass and then return up the steep mountain road.

Conchita was an outgoing child and everyone liked her. When the doctors tested her, they found her to be more intelligent that the other visionaries. It was, therefore, concluded that she was the leader.

Conchita helped her mother with the daily chores. Our Lady had told her that fidelity in ordinary life is very pleasing to God. We must make sacrifices out of the "little things."

Our Lady taught the girls the simple virtues of humility, obedience, purity, prayer and charity. She also stressed the value of patience, especially with the little things. Conchita was a model for all of these virtues. People loved to be near her because she was so kind, and the graces she had received seemed to draw people to her.

Perhaps Conchita's first sacrifice was that of cutting her hair. When she was in Santandar, the authorities decided that she must have her hair cut. They gave many various reasons; she was too pretty, her hair was too long, it made her too noticeable, her long braids hypnotized the other girls, her hair made her stand out too much, and she should be more humble. Conchita was humble and obedient, but she did ask Our Lady later if she thought her hair looked nice.

Conchita's mother was not happy with the way her daughter had been treated when she was taken to Santandar to discuss the apparitions. The men were very rude to her and tried to keep them apart. She was surprised at how they would twist things and try to deceive her.

Dr. Pinal, one of the commissioners, said to Conchita, "If you don't deny seeing apparitions, people will think you are crazy and put you in an asylum!"

Conchita said nothing.

"Listen, Conchita," threatened the Doctor. "We will put your parents and your family in jail!"

"But I did see the Blessed Virgin," answered Conchita.

"If you retract yourself, you will be considered a lady, and we could have you admitted to a fine school. We will pay for it all."

They tried to get Conchita and her mother to sign papers saying that the apparitions were false and made up. The twelve-year-old girl was interrogated alone for hours, without her mother's knowledge.

Conchita and her mother always held the utmost regard for the clergy and treated them with great respect. However, in this case, Conchita's mother believed that the best thing to do for her daughter was to take her home. In spite of the protests from the authorities, she brought Conchita back to Garabandal.

Conchita's brother Miguel was six years older than she. He believed in the apparitions as soon as he heard about them because he knew that his sister was truthful.

He would follow the girls when they were in ecstasy, in order to protect them from the crowds, but many times they would move at such a rapid rate that he was unable to keep up with them.

He was horrified that people would shine big lights or hold matches up to the girls eyes. When he saw them sticking pins into the girls and burning them with matches he would make them stop. He was surprised that the girls never felt any discomfort while in ecstasy.

One day Conchita gave Miguel a new medal which he put on immediately. She told him that when the priest came, he should have it blessed. Later in the evening, Conchita went into ecstasy. Their home was full of people who had given her many rosaries, medals and scapulars to be kissed by the Virgin Mary.

Miguel was in the corner of the room, and as he watched his sister, he thought about the medal she had given him. He wished that he had given it to her to be kissed. He no sooner had the thought when Conchita went over to him and took the medal off of his neck and presented to Our Lady to be kissed. She then put the medal back on her brother.

For a more spiritual sacrifice, one winter night Conchita left her home and walked around the village in a terrible snowstorm, saying the rosary. As people from the village heard her pass by their homes, they too got dressed and joined the child in prayer. Most of the villagers were up at three o'clock in the morning, walking in a snowstorm, saying the rosary!

Conchita tried to explain how it felt during and after an apparition: "A very great peace and happiness filled my soul during the apparition. After the Blessed Virgin left, it was like coming out of Heaven, and I would be filled with the desire to love the Heart of Jesus and Mary and tell the people about them, for this is the only thing that can make us happy."

At the beginning of 1966, Conchita and her mother went to Rome. Conchita was interviewed by members of the Sacred Congregation of the Faith and also had a meeting with Pope Paul VI where he said to her, "I bless you and, with me, the whole Church blesses you."

Conchita and her mother also visited the famous stigmatist, Padre Pio. The two had an unusual understanding between them, for they both loved Our Lady very much.

After the apparitions ended for her, Conchita went to the convent school of the Discalced Carmelite Missionary Sisters in 1966. There she claims she had a locution from Our Lord telling her that it was not His will that she become a nun.

> *I chose you in the world so that you would remain in it, experiencing the many difficulties you would encounter because of Me. I want all this for your sanctification and so that you may offer it for the salvation of the world. You must talk to the world about Mary. Wherever you are, you will find a cross and suffering.*

Conchita moved to New York on March 18, 1972, to work as a nurse in a clinic for Spanish speaking people. She felt the need to help other people as much as she could. She was kind and gentle, and the people loved her and respected her.

On May 26, 1973, Conchita married Patrick J. Keena of New York. They were married at Our Lady of Hope Church in Manhattan. Mari Loli, who had also moved to the United States, was her maid of honor. Conchita gave her crucifix, the one Our Lady kissed and Padre Pio blessed, to her husband Patrick, as a wedding gift.

Conchita soon became an American citizen. She and

Patrick have four children, three girls and a boy. Conchita teaches her children to love God and His Holy Mother.

Once a week, usually on Fridays, there is a Holy Hour for priests at Conchita's home. Priests and lay people gather to pray for priests as Our Blessed Mother requested so many years ago.

Since the apparitions, Conchita tried to live her life in accordance with what she has learned from Our Lady. That is, to live each moment of the day doing everything for God and offering up everything to Him. She tries to do everything to the best of her ability for the greater glory of God. Conchita says that you can fulfill the message anywhere. You can always be good and praise God.

Conchita says that she has often been asked about her feelings and the only way she can express them is by saying she felt great joy which cannot be explained in human terms. Even years later when Conchita speaks of the Blessed Virgin Mary her face radiates with a glow of love that is hard to describe. In seeing her, one can easily sense the deep emotions she still feels.

Conchita and her family still live in New York. Recently she sold her family home in Garabandal to a couple from Florida. The couple has experienced both spiritual and physical healing from their many years of devotion to Our Lady of Garabandal. They realize what a privilege it is to have a home where Our Lady appeared and they want to be in Garabandal when the miracle happens.

Conchita belongs to a number of prayer groups and welcomes visitors into her home to pray. She does not think that she is special in any way. "I pray that they all understand that it means nothing at all to meet or talk with me. They would be so much better off sitting in church quietly and listening to God."

Conchita has lived the messages of Garabandal her whole life and has led an exemplarily life of a Christian wife, mother, neighbor, and friend. She tries to keep focused on God throughout the day. At fifty years old, she is now enjoying being a grandmother since her oldest daughter is married and has two small children.

MARI LOLI—MARIA DOLORES MAZON

In the beginning, Conchita and Mari Loli had about the same number of apparitions. After April of 1963, Mari Loli's visions decreased along with the other girls, as Conchita's increased.

Mari Loli is the second of six children. Her father, Ceferino Mazon was the mayor of Garabandal. He had a small cafe where the men of the village gathered to talk. The other villagers looked up to Ceferino as an authority figure.

Mari Loli was quiet and obedient and helped her mother with the housework and other chores. What Mari Loli liked most was to care for her baby sister, Guadelupe.

Mari Loli's father liked to tell the story about when he heard Mari Loli get up and get dressed one winter night when there was a terrible snowstorm.

"Where are you going?" he asked the child.

"The Virgin is calling me to the lane," she replied.

"What if a wolf jumps out and gets you? Aren't you afraid?" asked Ceferino.

"No," said Mari Loli. "The Virgin will protect me."

"Do what you want, but neither your mother nor I will go with you," said her father. "It is too stormy."

He explained that one of them would always go with their daughter when she had these night callings because they were afraid that something would happen to her. He said that if he had been sure that it was the Virgin Mary he would not have worried so much about his daughter, but since he was not sure, one of them always accompanied her.

"We can't let her go out alone," said Mari Loli's mother as she began to get dressed.

"I'll go with you, but we must hurry. She has already left the house," said Ceferino.

They found their daughter on her knees in ecstasy. The snow was falling all around her as she knelt. They hurried to her side.

"She will freeze out here! It's so cold!" said Ceferino as he began to rub her cheeks.

To his great surprise, the child was warm. She appeared to have no discomfort at all. The parents stayed with their daughter for over an hour. They were cold and uncomfortable, and being outside at that late hour in a snowstorm was a big sacrifice for them to make.

They stayed for the love of their child and for the love of the Virgin. Although they often doubted, unexplainable occurrences became very normal for them.

Mari Loli's mother, Julia Mazon, said that when she looked at her daughter while in ecstasy she saw that her face changed entirely, and she felt as if the child were not her own. She did not understand the feeling of being so alone.

On another cold, winter night, Mari Loli's mother followed her as she went through the village on her knees in ecstasy. Julia was so afraid that Mari Loli would be hurt or get sick. She worried so much that her constant prayer was "Oh Lord, nothing else!"

Julia was terribly upset this particular evening, and she finally hid herself in a dark corner and began to cry. "Oh Blessed Mother," she prayed. "I cannot stand this any longer. Do not allow my daughter to continue dragging herself on her knees. She will be hurt."

Some villagers were following Mari Loli, and they heard her say, "You say my mother is crying! Oh, my mother is crying!"

The villagers found Julia and comforted her as much as they could until she and Mari Loli were able to walk home together.

Mari Loli's visions stopped completely on January 20, 1963, but she had several locutions after the apparitions.

Mari Loli and Jacinta went to a boarding school at the Sisters of Charity in Zaragoza, Spain. On October 24, 1965, one month after she was at the school, Mari Loli had a locution from the Blessed Virgin.

She told her many things and tried to comfort her, but the most important part of the locution for Mari Loli was when Our Lady said, *"You will have many doubts about all you have seen and heard from my mouth. Remember that I am always with you."*

Mari Loli asked Our Lady for a cross so she could suffer for priests.

"Endure everything with patience, be humble, recite the rosary every day, and pray for priests," was her response.

Mary Loli's suffering is sometimes physical but is more often interior mental pain. The denials and contradictions constantly plague her. Even as an adult she becomes confused and full of fear of sinning of either telling people about the apparitions or not telling them, depending upon her frame of mind at the time. The constant turmoil has been a heavy cross for her.

The Blessed Virgin told Mari Loli that it would please her very much if she recited the fifteen mysteries of the rosary every day for the conversion of all the sinners of the world.

Mari Loli said that she was faithful in saying the fifteen decades for a while, but then gradually she stopped saying so many rosaries. She explains that Our Lady must have known that she needed help, so she sent someone into her life to help her fulfill her wish.

On February 2, 1974, Mari Loli and Francis Lafleur were married in Brockton, Massachusetts. Francis had been saying the fifteen decades of the Rosary every day for quite some time, and, of course, he and his wife continue this practice together.

Francis had also always worn the Brown Scapular of Our Lady of Mt. Carmel. Mari Loli had worn the scapular too, but later had changed and wore the medal. Now the entire Lafleur family wears the Brown Scapular of

Our Lady of Mt. Carmel.

Mari Loli said in an interview in 1987, after she was an adult, that on the "night of the screams: they saw a great multitude of people who were suffering very much and screaming in anguish. There was fire all around, and when people ran toward the sea, they found the water was also burning. When the mothers were seen lifting up their babies, the three little girls screamed, "No! No! Not the children! Spare them!"

The Blessed Virgin explained to the little girls that a great tribulation could take place. There would be a time when the Church would appear to be on the verge of disappearing and would experience a great trial! Priests would have to go into hiding, and it would be difficult for them to say Mass.

When the girls asked Our Lady the name of the great tribulation, she said it was Communism. She said that Communism would spread all over the world. Mari Loli said that the Tribulation would come before the Warning, the Miracle and the Chastisement.

In July of 1988, the Lafleur family (Mari Loli, her husband, Francis, and their three children, Francis Jr., Melanie and Maria Dolores) met Pope John Paul II during a semi-private audience. The Holy Father knew that Mari Loli was one of the Garabandal visionaries.

Mari Loli's husband kissed the Holy Father's ring, and the Holy Father kissed the two little daughters of the visionary. Young Francis told the Pope that he wanted to become a priest and asked the Pope to pray for him. The Holy Father assured the boy that he would pray for him. He blessed the whole family.

Young Francis did go into the seminary for a few years but has since graduated from college with a degree in business. The family still lives in Massachusetts but they return to Garabandal whenever possible. During the summer of 1998 Mari Loli visited Garabandal and stayed with her sister who has remained in the village. Her dear friend,

Jacinta, also spent the summer in Garabandal with her family. The two women enjoyed each others company as they walked along the quaint roads of the village and visited the familiar sites where so many wonderful apparitions occurred so long ago. They both spent time greeting pilgrims and answering questions but mostly they shared their experiences again with each other and renewed their own faith in the apparitions.

None of the visionaries have made any plans to be in Garabandal during the warning or the miracle, but have completely left it up to God. "If God and Our Blessed Mother want us there, then we will be there." They always try to do the will of God.

JACINTA

Jacinta is the second to the youngest of eight children. There are four boys and four girls in the family. Jacinta and Conchita are cousins, their grandmothers are sisters.

Jacinta's parents were among the most poverty stricken in the village. Her father worked hard, and her mother, Maria Gonzalez, was very fervent in her religion. They devoted themselves to their family and their Church.

Jacinta's mother had the privilege of being the woman who would go through the village each evening at twilight and ring the bell to remind the people to pray for the poor souls. When she became too sick to do this, she passed the bell on to her first cousin, Aniceta, Conchita's mother.

Jacinta's parents always showed patience and kindness to the many visitors who came to their home daily to witness the apparitions and to see their daughter. The family had no peace because of the constant flow of people. Even during mealtime and late at night, people would come to visit.

Jacinta's father, Simon, was very protective of his little daughter. He believed her immediately and said that every apparition he witnessed moved him deeply.

Jacinta's mother would accompany Jacinta to the various apparitions no matter what time it was, day or night. She believed in the apparitions and spoke of her personal proof when one night Jacinta was going alone, in ecstasy, to the cemetery to bless the dead. The girls often did this, but on that particular night, Jacinta's mother was very uncomfortable going out alone, in the dark, to the cemetery at night. Silently, in her heart, she was wishing that her friend, Angelita, was going with her.

Suddenly she saw Jacinta stop. The child turned and changed her direction and went directly to Angelita's house and knocked on the door. Of course, Angelita accompanied them to the cemetery. Jacinta's mother said that only Our Lady could have read her heart and guided Jacinta so that she would have peace.

Another personal sign for Jacinta's family was the child's ability to say by heart the Litany of Our Lady of Loreto. She had never been taught this prayer and said that Our Lady had taught it to her once. She could also recite the mysteries of the rosary, and she had not known them before the apparitions began.

Jacinta had fewer visions than Conchita and Mari Loli but more than Mari Cruz. She did not know why the Blessed Virgin did not appear to her as much as some of the others.

Jacinta's mother, Maria, going through the streets ringing a bell to remind the townsfolk to pray for the dead, a time-honored custom in the village.

At times she felt that it was a punishment because Our Lady told her once that she should obey her parents. Perhaps it was because Our Lady knew that Jacinta's mother needed rest, and she was just being gentle and kind to them in another way.

Jacinta always knew that Our Lady loved her very much. She said that the Blessed Virgin talked with her about everything, the way a mother would talk to her daughter.

Our Lady asked for penance and sacrifice, and Jacinta believes this means to accept the difficult things, the things you do not like. Our Lady said that we should be simple, honest and obedient, and Jacinta's life has been a good example of these virtues.

On June 23, 1962, Mari Loli and Jacinta wrote the following together:

> The Blessed Virgin told us that the world goes on without the least improvement. There will be few who will see God; there are so few that it causes the Blessed Virgin much distress!
>
> What a pity they do not change! The Blessed Mother told us that the Chastisement is coming. Because people do not improve their ways, the cup is filling up. How sad the Virgin was! Although she did not want to show it because she loves us so much, she bears that suffering alone because she is so good.
>
> Be good, all of you, so as to please the Virgin. She told us that the good people should pray for the bad. Yes, let us pray to Almighty God for the whole world, for all those who do not know her.
>
> Be good, very good, all of you.
>
> Maria Dolores Mazon (age 13)
Jacinta Gonzalez   (age 13)

After Jacinta no longer received apparitions, she would go with the other girls when they were in ecstasy. She noticed that when she had been in ecstasy, no matter how long the visions lasted, she always felt refreshed when they were over. When she no longer saw the Virgin, she would get very tired as she watched the other girls.

Jacinta was the only one of the visionaries to mention a vision of the Sacred Heart of Jesus. She said that He remained much more ingrained in her mind. He had a look of love on His face, and although he did not say anything, she felt he was saying, *"I am with you, and I will always be with you."*

The vision of the Sacred Heart became a great comfort for Jacinta. Even when she had doubts about seeing the Blessed Virgin, she never had doubts about seeing the Sacred Heart. She was always absolutely sure about that vision.

For a long time Jacinta felt that she should become a nun. Many people told her she should since she had seen Our Lady. Jacinta often asked Our Lady but the Virgin never answered her question. Jacinta realized that we must all follow our own vocations and live up to what we are supposed to do.

Jacinta married Jeffrey Monihan, a young American Navy man, who was stationed in Spain. She was the only visionary to be married in the Church of San Sebastian of Garabandal. Jeff was the perfect mate for Jacinta because he had been groomed by Father Aloysius Ellacuria C.M.F. Jeff had worked for Father Aloysius as his personal secretary and driver and Father Aloysius was his friend and spiritual director.

Father Aloysius was a very holy priest who had been given many special gifts of the Holy Spirit, including the ability to read the soul. He said the gift was given to him to help people and he used it to help people make good confessions and to counsel them. He also had the gift of healing and was very well known for his healing ministry. Father always said it was God who did the work, and he, Father Aloysius, was just the instrument.

Father Aloysius visited Garabandal in 1970 and was very impressed. Later, when he met the visionaries, he read their souls and found truth in all of their visions. Of course, he was very happy when Jacinta and Jeff were married. He told Jacinta, "Jeff didn't know his vocation in life, but when he married you, his eyes were opened. He told Jeff that Jacinta's soul was "very special." They attribute the miracle of the birth of their daughter, Maria to the intercession of Father Aloysius.

Jacinta has received some special gifts too. She has prophetic dreams and often knows when things are going to happen before they actually occur. On the morning of January 7, 1979, Jacinta woke up and told Jeff her dream of his father's death and funeral. She described everything to him and was very sad. Jeff's father was a dentist in California and was in very good health. Later that day, they received a phone call that he had died suddenly of a heart attack. The funeral was exactly as Jacinta had predicted. There had been other similar instances where she will know what is going to happen. Thanks to Father Aloysius, they are able to understand these special gifts and use them for the glory of God.

Jacinta leads a very deep spiritual life. She is the picture of humility. She belongs to a number of rosary prayer groups but prefers to pray alone or with her husband and child. She said that if she could give a message to the world, she would say, "People should have mutual respect for each other as human beings, and above all they should place God first before their fellow man."

Jacinta also keeps a diary, but she says that it is very personal and intimate and is not meant for public use. Perhaps it will be published after her death.

MARI CRUZ

Mari Cruz was the youngest of the visionaries. She was only eleven years old when the apparitions began. She had fewer apparitions than the other girls and was the first to stop seeing Our Lady.

On August 8, 1961, Our Lady taught Mari Cruz how to pray. The child was kneeling at the altar of Our Lady of the Rosary in the Church of San Sebastian. She had walked there in ecstacy from the pines with the other girls. They had stopped seeing the vision outside the church, but this was an especially long trance for Mari Cruz.

Mari Cruz began to recite the Creed very slowly. She said that Our Lady recited the prayer first, and then she said the words after her. Then she recited the Hail Holy Queen very slowly. She also taught the child how to make the Sign of the Cross properly and with reverence.

"Now, I know better how to pray, but before, I was better at playing," said Mari Cruz.

She also saw the Infant Jesus. Mari Cruz was heard speaking with Our Lady, "I'm so glad the Infant Jesus has come! It's been so long since He came! Why have you waited so long before coming to me, and why do you come more often to the three others?"

Mari Cruz means "Mary of the Cross" and the child had much to suffer, just as Mary did at the Cross of Christ. The most difficult struggle for Mari Cruz was when she was denied the privilege of seeing Our Lady. She suffered throughout the time of the apparitions when the other girls saw the Blessed Virgin and she did not.

This fact, would often cause the people of the village to make very cruel comments concerning the child's holiness and faith. As a result, she would often be ridiculed.

"Why doesn't the Virgin like you as much as the others?" jeered some people.

"What have you done so that the Virgin won't appear to you?" asked others.

"You must be so bad that Our Lady doesn't like you anymore," taunted someone else.

These cruel remarks deeply hurt the child. She did not understand and had no explanations for what had happened. She would try to offer these special sufferings up to God.

Mari Cruz's parents also suffered because of the apparitions. Sometimes they did not believe in them and did not want their daughter involved. They were very poor, and the crowds of people who came to the village throughout the day and night would often be rude and inconsiderate and would disturb the well-being of the family.

Many times Mari Cruz's parents would tell her not to go with the other girls. Our Lady always stressed obedience and reminded the girls that they should obey their parents before they obeyed her. Perhaps it was out of kindness that Our Lady stopped appearing to the child first, but Mari Cruz did not feel that way about it.

Although Mari Cruz could not convince her parents about the apparitions, she was very instrumental in convincing Mari Loli's mother.

One day Mari Loli's house was packed with people. Her mother, Julia, had been caring for the baby when she heard more noises. She started downstairs, but the house was so packed she could not get down. The people said that Mari Cruz was in ecstacy and that she was coming to their home.

"Most Blessed Virgin, if this is true, out of all the people who are here, may Mari Cruz give me, and only me, the crucifix to kiss," prayed Julia silently, for she was beginning to have doubts, and she felt that she needed proof again.

She stood in the middle of the stairs, and Mari Cruz went right to her and gave her the crucifix to kiss. She was the only one. Julia knew her prayer had been answered.

Mari Cruz stopped seeing Our Lady on September 12, 1962, four months before the apparitions stopped for Mari Loli and Jacinta.

Deeply hurt, Mari Cruz tried to simulate the ecstasies, but it was impossible. This act in itself proved that she had not been faking the original apparitions. Feelings of doubt and denial filled her. She has been tormented and confused and has retracted most of her statements on and off for years as to what actually happened.

On May 2, 1970, Mari Cruz became the first of the four visionaries to get married. She married Ignacio Caballero from Aviles and moved near the coast of Spain. They have four children; Ignacio Manuel, Maria de Lourdes, Juan Carlos and Mari Crux.

Mari Cruz has been plagued with doubts and confusions about the visions more than any of the other visionaries. At times she would deny seeing the Blessed Virgin but then when asked she was able to describe her perfectly. She is a very sensitive woman and for years decided that it was easier to just not talk about the apparitions and to avoid people. She avoided talking about Garabandal to anyone except her family and very close, personal friends. She has stayed in close contact with the other three visionaries.

By 1999, it seems as if she has finally found her inner peace and she has accepted the fact that she saw the Blessed Virgin when she was a child. She has begun to come out of her shell and is more confident about herself. As a child, Mari Cruz was often judged harshly by the visitors who came to the village and she was sometimes described as the "homely one." Mari Cruz would often ask Our Blessed Mother to make her more beautiful. Indeed, her prayers have been answered, for she has become a very dignified and attractive looking woman. Like Conchita, Mari Cruz speaks of the joy she felt, and her face radiates the beauty of heaven when she now speaks of the Blessed Virgin Mary. "It is true," she says quietly. She prays with her family and now has a rosary group in her home.

CHAPTER 14

Garabandal Today

When Our Lady apparently appeared to the four young girls in Garabandal, Spain from June 18, 1961, until June 18, 1965, she stressed the importance of her messages for the world.

On October 18, 1961

You must make many sacrifices, perform much penance, and visit the Blessed Sacrament frequently. But first, you must lead good lives. If you do not, a chastisement will befall you. The cup is already filling up, and if people do not change, a very great chastisement will come upon them.

On June 18, 1965

As my message of October 18 has not been complied with and has not been made known to the world, I am advising you that this is the last one. Before, the cup was filling up. Now it is flowing over. Many cardinals, many bishops and many priests are on the road to perdition and are taking many souls with them.

Less and less importance is being given to the Eucharist. You should turn the wrath of God

*away from yourselves by your efforts. If you ask
His forgiveness with sincere hearts, He will
pardon you.*

*I, your mother, through the intercession of
Saint Michael the Archangel, ask you to amend
your lives. You are now receiving the last warnings. I love you very much and do not want your
condemnation. Pray to us with sincerity, and we
will grant your requests. You should make more
sacrifices. Think about the passion of Jesus.*

These were very serious messages but the people of the
world in the 1960s did not pay attention to them. The
authorities in Spain were more interested in proving that
the girls were not telling the truth than in spreading the
messages.

The Church continued to study the issue, neither af-
firming nor condemning the apparitions. When the girls
began to have their own doubts and denials, people did
not recognize this as the manifestation of the first
prophesy and, instead, turned away from believing in the
apparitions and spreading the messages. The result of this
confusion was that the majority of the world was ignorant
of these important apparitions and deprived from knowing and receiving the messages alledgedly given by Our
Lady at Garabandal.

It is important to note that at no time has the Church
ever condemned the apparitions at Garabandal, although
the rumor has popped up time and again. The Church
has always been open to the study of Garabandal. Our
Holy Father has met with the girls and has apparently
been favorably impressed.

There is an enormous contrast between the village of
Garabandal, Spain and the fast paced modern world of
today. The people of Garabandal have held firmly to their
faith. The people who witnessed the visionaries during
their visions have never doubted and have firmly believed

in the apparitions of Our Lady and follow the teachings of her messages.

They have continued to pray the rosary every day, both in the Church and at home with their families. Each evening a woman still walks through the village ringing the bell to remind the people to pray for the poor souls in Purgatory. When the church bells ring at noon, the people stop their work and say the Angelus. They pray, make sacrifices, perform much penance, and they lead very good simple lives. They have a deep respect for the Church and the Sacraments.

The people continue to have reverence and respect for God and the Holy Eucharist. Many people believe that the miracle of the Eucharist, which they witnessed, has brought them to a deeper understanding and love for the Real Presence of Jesus Christ in the Blessed Sacrament.

Jacinta said, "The apparitions helped to increase the spirituality and faith of the people in the village. Our Lady did not come just for the people in the village of Garabandal, but rather, she came for the whole world, for all of mankind."

In the fast paced, more modern world, people have lost sight of holy reverence toward God and often do not have time for prayer. Churches have become "multi-purpose" rooms with tabernacles placed in small chapels or dark corners. Respect for the Blessed Sacrament is at an all-time low. For some, the Sacraments have become mere symbols and have lost their true meaning.

At Garabandal, Our Lady warned us of these dangers. She talked about trials and tribulations of the Church and the world and predicted the warning, miracle, and chastisement that could be alleviated if mankind would pray and turn away from sin. She said in 1961 that the cup is already filling up, and if we do not change, a very great chastisement will come upon us. In 1965, Our Lady again warned, *"Before, the cup was filling up. Now it is flowing over."*

We are now living in the times of Garabandal. Many believe the warning, miracle and chastisement will come, and we must be prepared for them. The warning could be very frightening for those who do not understand. The visionaries have explained the warning the best way that they know how, but there are still many questions to be answered. The best preparation is prayer, fasting and frequent Confession and Holy Communion.

Without knowing about the apparitions of Garabandal and the messages of Our Lady, people will be extremely frightened and confused when the warning occurs. Those who know about the warning will realize that another prophesy of Garabandal is being fulfilled. They will understand that the miracle at the pines will soon take place. Instead of being a frightening experience, it will become one of hope.

It is stated that the miracle will take place sometime within a year after the warning. Once the predicted miracle occurs, at the pines area, Garabandal will become a major Marian Shrine and place of prayer and devotion.

The messages state the severity of the chastisement is conditional. It depends upon the response of mankind to the messages of the Blessed Virgin. It will come directly from God, Who is all just.

We must have faith and trust in Jesus and Mary as they go about their work to carry out God's plan. It is in God's plan for the Blessed Virgin Mary to come to earth to help her children. She loves us and wants to present us to the Father. The warning, miracle and chastisement are predicted, but she does not want us to live in fear; she wants us to live her messages. Prayer (especially the rosary), fasting, wearing the Brown Scapular of Mount Carmel, the Eucharist, Confession and reflection on the passion of Christ will obtain for us the divine help we need to avoid sin and become good, holy people on the path to Eternal Salvation.

We must remember what Our Lady told Conchita on her last visit:

Conchita, I have not come for your sake alone. I have come for all my children, so that I may draw them closer to our Hearts...I have to tell you, it (the message) *is for your own good, and, if you all fulfill it, for the Glory of God. I love you all very much, and I desire your salvation and to gather you all here in Heaven with the Father, the Son and the Holy Spirit.*

Bibliography

Francois, Robert, *O Children Listen to Me,* The Workers of Our Lady of Mt. Carmel, P.O. Box 606, Lindenhurst, New York, 1982.

Karminski, Stanley, "Our Lady at Garabandal," *Mary's People,* April, May 1991.

Karminski, Stanley, "Garabandal," *Signs of the Times,* Vol. 3 No. 3, July, Aug., Sept., 1991.

Laffineur, M. and Pelletier, M. T. *Star on the Mountain,* Our Lady of Mt. Carmel of Garabandal, Inc., Newtonville, NY, 1974.

Nevins, Albert, *The Maryknoll Catholic Dictionary,* Dimension Books, New York, 1965.

Perez, Ramon, *Garabandal, the Village Speaks,* The Workers of Our Lady of Mt. Carmel, Inc., Lindenhurst, NY, 1985.

Pelletier, Joseph A., *Garabandal, Prayer and the Rosary,* Assumption Publication, Worcester, MA, 1970.

Pelletier, Joseph A., *God Speaks at Garabandal,* Assumption Publication, Worcester, MA, 1970.

Pelletier, Joseph A., *Our Lady Comes to Garabandal,* Assumption Publication, Worcester, MA, 1974.

Sanchez-Ventura Y Pascual, *The Apparitions of Garabandal,* St. Michael's Garabandal Center, Pasadena, CA, 1989.

Saint Joseph Edition of the New American Bible, Catholic Book Publishing Co., New York, 1970.

Garabandal Magazine, issues from 1979 through 1991, The Workers of Our Lady of Mount Carmel, P.O. Box 606, Lindenhurst, NY 11757.

Moynihan, Jeffrey, Father Aloysius: *Wonder Worker in American,* Queenship Publishing Co., Santa Barbara, CA, 1996.

In 1991, Bishop Jose Vilaplaua, the Bishop of Santander, presented to the Congregation for the Doctrine of the Faith the study of the alleged apparitions at Garabandal in which it was concluded that there was no evidence of supernatural validity to the apparitions. He asked for pastoral direction concerning the case. On November 18, 1992, the Congregation replied by stating there was no need for direct intervention by the Holy See to take away the jurisdiction of the ordinary bishop of Santander in this case. The bishop then released the following statement on October 11, 1996, concerning the alleged apparitions at Garabandal, which agreed with all of his predecessors since 1961: "I accept the decision of my predecessors and I agree with the direction of the Holy See. In reference to the Eucharistic celebration in Garabandal, following the decision of my predecessors, I ruled that Masses can be celebrated only in the parish church and there will be no references to the alleged apparitions and visiting priests who want to say Mass must have approval from the pastor, who has my authorization. It's my wish that this information is helpful to you."

The Church has neither approved nor condemned the apparitions at Garabandal. It is viewed as a private revelation and the Church allows the followers to have the freedom of belief. At no time does the Church demand that one should believe in private revelation because the Church teaches that Sacred Tradition and Sacred Scripture make up the single sacred deposit of the Word of God.

Those who have followed the messages of Garabandal see the response of the Bishop as another fulfillment of Our Lady's prophecies. She predicated that shortly before the warning something would occur which would make many people turn away from believing in Garabandal. She also predicted there would be a bishop who would not believe in the events at first but he would believe after the Blessed Virgin gave him a sign. The real proof of the apparitions at Garabandal will occur with the warning, miracle and possible chastisement. It has been predicted that at that time everyone will believe.